Champion of the Great American Family

★

Champion of
the Great American
Family

★

by
Congresswoman
Pat Schroeder
with Andrea Camp and Robyn Lipner

Random House New York

Library of Congress Cataloging-in-Publication Data
Schroeder, Patricia.
Champion of the great American family.
Includes index.
1. Family—United States. 2. Working mothers—United States. 3. Schroeder, Patricia.
4. Women legislators—United States—Biography.   I. Title.
HQ536.S37   1989   306.8'5'0973   88-42682
ISBN 0-394-56574-6

Manufactured in the United States of America

*To Jim, for giving up home-cooked meals,
darned socks, and a dust-free home*

Acknowledgments

This book would still be scribbled notes on napkins, pizza boxes, and message pads were it not for the time and help of my family and friends in Colorado and Washington, D.C. Our dog, Wolfie, cooperated by not eating the notes.

The book was a family effort. Jim, Scott, Jamie, my mother and father, my brother, Mike, and his family all pitched in.

I would also like to thank Andrea Camp and Robyn Lipner, who helped me to reconstruct my legislative life, and my editor, Charlotte Mayerson, who shepherded the book from start to finish.

A very special thanks to Linda Ittner, who was my legislative assistant from 1974 to 1985, when she died of leukemia. Linda was an indefatigable and imaginative advocate for family policy.

Contents

Champion of
the Great American
Family

1

Focus on the Family

WHAT began on June 5, 1987, as an exciting quest for the presidency of the United States ended three months later, on September 28, as a search for Kleenex.

Even as that Monday in September started I could feel the effects of the hectic schedule of the last few days: Washington, D.C., in the Congress, on Thursday; California on Friday; back in Washington on the red-eye Saturday morning for the Congressional Black Caucus Presidential Candidate Forum; and, finally, home to Colorado Saturday night to prepare for my Monday announcement. I'd been living at that pace all summer, hermetically sealed in an airplane, eating terrible food, going without sleep. I have always tried to be flexible in both my personal and my political life. "Make the most of opportunities as they come up" is my motto. But the demands for spontaneity in the summer of 1987 would have been a challenge for anybody.

Entering the presidential primary race had been, earlier in the year, the farthest thing from my mind. Instead, I was focusing on preparing a speech I was to give at the University of Minnesota, my alma mater. But then my fellow Coloradan Gary Hart, whose campaign I was cochairing, made a stupid and costly mistake. After daring the press to "go ahead and follow me"—and thus prove that his reputation as a womanizer was false—he was caught in a compromising association with Donna Rice.

After the Hart furor subsided—while my husband, Jim, was in Thailand on business and my son, Scott, at school in England—friends and supporters began to urge me to take a look at the race. Then in June, less than a month after Hart dropped out, my "look at the race" exploded on the front page of *The New York Times*, on the hourly television news reports, and in newspapers and magazines across the country.

The questions other candidates had considered much earlier and in private I began to explore publicly, under bright lights, in a process that was for me a great, though extremely challenging, experience. I was grilled by editorial boards, cheered by crowds, and evaluated by political pundits. I was running as Patricia Schroeder, a member of Congress with fifteen years' experience, but automatically I was seen as Everywoman, advancing the struggle of women for a stronger voice in government. Like it or not, my potential candidacy for the highest elected office in our country was going to be a hook for America-watchers, political analysts, and newspaper columnists to appraise the progress of women in this country. I countered their probing questions with my own opinion that "America is man enough to back a woman."

A few months later, on that Monday at Denver's Civic Center, I was anxious to get onstage and come clean to my supporters. It was time to tie up the loose ends of the campaign. I was ready to get back to the job I love—being the congresswoman for Denver. Jim, my husband of twenty-five years, knew I had been leaning against continuing in the race. He had been hustling all the legal expertise and political acumen he could, to try to convince me to run. He would pace around our kitchen floor, smoking his pipe, playing out various political scenarios, and making a Schroeder presidency sound not only possible but plausible. I would then play devil's advocate and poke holes in his scenarios. I felt that I had been working without a net all summer. Jim was sure that if I kept at it, everything would fall into place. We did this dance several times during that last week before the decision. Jim's advocacy of my running was not limited to the kitchen. We debated in the car, in airplanes, over the phone, and at parties. And it was not limited to me. Jim would debate the question with friends, columnists, and my staff. People were stunned by his enthusiasm and confidence. They had expected him to be against the idea.

That might be a conventional husband's reaction, but as I will explain in the next chapter, my husband was responsible for my getting into politics in the first place. Back in 1972, when most people thought of the congressional race in Denver as a noble suicide mission for a Democrat, Jim convinced me to see it as an incredible challenge and an opportunity to present issues that needed discussion. Neither of us understood what the race would lead to.

Now, in the fall of 1987, Jim was trying again to persuade me, but this time the situation was more complicated and we were more sophisticated. I knew there were several factors that had to be in place before I could stage a confident run for the presidency. First, I needed a substantial amount of money—about two million dollars—so that I could wage and win a full-scale national campaign. (They didn't give discounts for latecomers!) I refused to conduct a campaign in the red. How could I go around the country speaking out against the national debt if I was running up a debt myself?

Second, I needed a cadre of savvy and creative organizers who could quickly put in place an effective and cost-efficient campaign and who would understand my direct style. Otherwise I'd end up with Potomac professionals who would spend their time trying to mold me into their idea of what a candidate should be.

I was entering the campaign way behind schedule. Could I jump-start the kind of organization other candidates had spent years assembling and planning? Further, I would run only if I thought I had a good chance to win. It would not be a symbolic campaign. There was a tendency, from the very beginning, for the press to categorize me as a "women's candidate." Would the country see me that way or view me as a presidential candidate who happened to be a woman? I did not want my gender to block my message.

My decision not to run was based on these political considerations. Many people were sure that my principal concern was what a presidential race would do to my kids, but this was not the case. My son, Scott, was in his senior year at Georgetown University. My daughter, Jamie, was about to enter her senior year at high school and start the rigorous exercise of applying to colleges. Although I would have liked to have time to help her, she assured me she could handle the problem on her own. My children have always been very poised and cool about my job. Jamie was two and Scott was six when I was first elected to Congress, and as they were growing up I tried to include them in my work whenever possible. Whether it was a child care demonstration or a Christmas party at the White House, arms talks in Europe, or a tour of the refugee camps in Thailand, we treated my job as a seminar. My children were encouraged to be a part of my political life—but only if they wanted to. There were no command performances. Scott and Jamie were used to being in the public eye and I doubted that the constant scrutiny of a presidential campaign would be too much for them. I asked them how they would handle it if the *National Enquirer* followed them when they went out on dates. Scott told me not to worry because lately the paper was only covering aliens from outer space who had discovered new diets!

However, when I looked at the situation early in the fall, I knew that I didn't have the pieces in place for the professional campaign I wanted to run. I had about one million dollars in the bank, but that was not enough to mount a credible nationwide campaign and to hire a top-notch staff. Further, while Americans are making progress toward accepting the idea of a woman president, women still don't "look presidential" to many voters. At least, I didn't. My laugh, my signature, my mannerisms, were seen as too feminine. I was told that in politics boyish charm is fine but girlish charm is out of place. People predicted that the first woman president would be a tough character, "weaned on a pickle"—in other words, just like a man. I hope they're wrong. I don't think men have a lock on the correct way to run the Oval Office. In fact, though women might not do a better job, they could hardly do it worse.

On his weekly television show, David Brinkley mentioned my rule "No dough, no go." Then he satirically observed that if I did not run because of lack of money, my example might change the course of American politics. Everyone felt that the "ego food" of the bright lights would always outweigh common sense. People fool themselves into thinking, Where there's a will, there's a way. There *is* a way—going heavily into debt. That is not my way. I had to keep reminding myself that I wanted common sense, not my ego, to be the driving force of my campaign.

In the end, my pragmatism prevailed. Walking onto the stage to address hundreds of supporters on that perfect September day in Denver, I knew the speech was going to be tricky. My message was a paradox: My summer exploration has been so successful that I am not going to run. I could see people scratching their heads. I wanted to make it clear that I had learned that the presidency was not necessarily out of my grasp, but that to win would take a lot more preparation and time and money than I had.

As I took a deep breath and approached the microphone, the crowds started chanting "Run, Pat, run." How could I guarantee that all those chanting people would understand that I valued their support so much that I couldn't pursue my dream at this time? I began my speech with a round of thank yous. That was easy. Out of the corner of my eye I could see my mom and dad, Bernice and Lee Scott, stoically standing by. My parents had been troupers throughout the summer. My father and my brother, Mike, had been my campaign organization in Iowa, making calls and contacts, working their heads off. (We lived in Des Moines during my high school years; my mother was a public school teacher and my father was in aviation insurance.)

They had been sure I would stay in the race. I had never backed down before—why should this be different? My dad was so sure that when a California vendor who had been supplying us with campaign buttons called and said she had heard rumors that I was not going to run, Dad laughed and said that was just a ploy to keep the press guessing.

When I reached the crucial part of my Denver speech and said that I would not be running for president, the crowd groaned. That's the only way to describe it. People shouted, "No, no," and began to chant again, "Run, Pat, run." I was unprepared for the crowd's powerful reaction. Those fabulous supporters had given up their summer weekends as well as their dollars to my campaign. I was honored and moved, but my heart sank.

I rarely show emotion in public. That day, I felt I was in command—sure of my decision and of the crowd's ultimate understanding. But when I heard the audience groan, I began to cry. I knew there that I had underestimated how much I wanted to pursue the presidency. I went on with my speech, but, I'm sorry to say, it was my tears, not my words, that got the headlines.

I later decided I could make my fortune marketing Schroeder teardrop jewelry or going on TV, like a tennis star, endorsing Kleenex tissues. One good result of my tears was that crying came out of the closet. The stories poured in. Washington superlawyer Joe Califano told me that during his farewell speech after President Jimmy Carter fired him from the Department of Health, Education, and Welfare, he cried uncontrollably. A constituent wrote and reminded me that President Lyndon B. Johnson sobbed through a civil rights ceremony at the White House. A lobbyist sent me the story of George Washington's farewell dinner with his revolutionary war generals, when there was hugging and crying all around the table.

For weeks afterward, there were columns pro and con my reaction. Some writers went so far as to say that my tears had dampened all hopes for women in presidential politics for the rest of this century! Meg Greenfield of *The Washington Post* invited me to give my perspective. In an article I wrote, I quoted Ted Sorensen, who had once introduced me as a politician who can "draft a bill, stir a crowd, fly a plane, bake a cake, pass a law, coin a phrase—and run for president." In my reply, I corrected Ted: "Wrong," I said. "I know a bakery that delivers." But in *The Washington Post* op-ed piece I added one other item to the list: "And wears her heart on her sleeve."

The critics who seemed most insane to me were those who said they wouldn't want the person who had a "finger on the button" to be someone who cries. I answered that I wouldn't want that person to be someone who *doesn't* cry.

The press furor overshadowed the valuable lessons I learned during the summer of 1987. Traveling across the country, I found that men and women, college students and the elderly, want politicians to understand what is going on in their lives. They want government policies to reflect that understanding. A woman from Florida wrote and thanked me for speaking directly to her. She said that she hadn't voted in the past two presidential elections, but that she would vote for me.

My summer campaign activated many people like that woman in Florida. Some had been politically aware but not politically active. Others had, in the past, been politically active but had been dropouts during the recent elections.

People wanted to feel that the candidate they backed understood them. Audiences asked questions about my personal life, as if to make sure I wasn't just spouting abstract rhetoric. They asked not only "How can women work and have a family?" but also "How did you, Pat Schroeder, work and have a family?"; not only "How do we increase child care options for families?" but also "What did you and your husband do about child care?" The questions made it clear to me that Americans are desperate to find answers that will help them juggle all the roles and chores modern life has laid upon them.

My concern for the American family was reinforced by my summer experiences. For example, on one August day during that hectic time, I gave a keynote speech on family issues twice in Portland, Oregon—to the National Women's Political Caucus and to the National Association of Postmasters of America. They were very different groups but they had similar reactions to the family speech.

The audience at the Women's Political Caucus responded enthusiastically, as might be expected. The postmasters' meeting began with the Lord's Prayer. The average age of the crowd was about fifty. The placards of the various delegations indicated that there was a heavy concentration from the Southern states. As I talked about the need for time off for parents to be with their babies, I could see heads nodding in agreement. I talked about how we no longer have many "empty nests." The new generation of young people may be better educated than their parents but they still cannot find jobs that pay well enough for them to move out of their parents' houses. Heads kept nodding. When I finished, there was a standing ovation—proof that my message about getting the government finally to help families was one that transcended geographic, generational, and socioeconomic lines.

People want the American family to thrive and they are deeply worried about it. As a politician and a legislator I know that the American family needs to be protected and encouraged. That is what motivated me to begin this book.

Most other countries of the developed world do much more to help families than we do *and* they have better statistics on divorce, infant mortality, and adolescent problems. I think there's a connection. Politicians have viewed family issues as worth mentioning in speeches but not worth addressing in policy. Colleagues have told me that family issues are too vague to mobilize a constituency. Others say that the right wing has stolen the family and we can't reclaim it.

I disagree. I think that people's everyday experiences are helping all of us to define family policy. I certainly know that my own experiences combining my congressional career with my family responsibilities prompted my activism. My travels during the

summer of 1987 and my 1988 Great American Family tour convinced me that the time has come for politicians to focus on a
national policy that reflects the realities of today's family life and
not the romanticism of the past.

This book will address the problems families face and how they
can be solved. The economic stress of maintaining the American
dream—house, car, college, health insurance, and the rest—has
driven many, many women out into the workplace and has sharp-
ened the conflict between the demands of work and the needs of
the family. The American people are justified in asking their
government for help with their problems. Other countries did
this long ago. We must now "play catch-up," and do it fast. Too
many of our families are hurting.

2

Every Mother Is a Working Mother

WHEN I first ran for Congress in 1972, as I have said, the chances for a successful Democratic candidacy in Denver did not look too good. Nationally, Richard Nixon was on his way to burying George McGovern in what was, at that time, the largest landslide victory in presidential election history.

In Denver, the prospects for a Democrat's winning the city's seat in Congress were so dim that no one wanted to run. Mike McKevitt, a popular Republican district attorney, had won the seat in 1970 after a bitter Democratic primary in which an antiwar challenger defeated the ten-term incumbent, thereby splitting the Democratic party. Worse, the 1971 redistricting had shifted a chunk of Democratic neighborhoods into an adjoining suburban district, thus improving McKevitt's chances.

A group of young, liberal Democrats, including my husband, caucused through the spring of 1972 to try to recruit a candidate. After a lot of discussion back and forth, the talk turned to running a woman. In the old days, there were two ways for a woman to run for Congress: as the widow of an incumbent or as challenger in a hopeless race. Scenario number two was how I was chosen to run.

Jim stayed out late one night and came home just as I was getting into bed. "Guess whose name came up as a candidate for Congress," he said.

"I don't know."

"Guess."

"I don't know," I said, slightly irritated.

Jim said, "Yours."

I stared at him blankly.

"Somebody's got to run in this one, Pat. And none of the men want to go for it. Larry Wright [a friend and a prominent Colorado Democrat] said, 'Let's run someone a little different. How about your wife, Jim?' "

"What did you say?" I asked.

" 'How about *your* wife?' "

I did end up running, but throughout the primary and the general race, I continued working at my part-time jobs teaching law, as hearing officer for Colorado's state personnel system, and as a volunteer counsel for Planned Parenthood. I spent little time wondering what life as a congresswoman would be like. There didn't seem to be much point. The one trip we made to Washington to raise money and support from the Democratic National Committee had been fruitless. I wanted to run a campaign on the issues—the Vietnam War, housing, the environment, children, the elderly. The DNC didn't think I would win that way—or any way—and they sent us home empty-handed.

So we raised money the same way we organized, at the grass roots. We had thousands of campaign posters printed on bright-colored paper because we "got a deal." It turned out that the bright colors were almost as controversial as the posters themselves. Few candidates defy the unspoken rule that campaign literature be printed in red, white, and blue, and that it show the candidate in front of the Capitol dome, with his family and the dog. (Republicans would always insert a horseback shot in their brochures, and the Democrats a bike-riding scene, to show their love of the outdoors.) Not only was the color of our paper unorthodox, my face didn't appear on any of my posters. Instead, one poster showed a field of tombstones in Arlington Cemetery with the headline "Yes, some American troops have already been withdrawn from Vietnam." Another had a picture of a young Hispanic child with the caption "This radical troublemaker wants something from you. Hope."

I discovered early in that first campaign that I enjoyed talking to people one-on-one, and I did a lot of it. Because they thought victory was a sure thing, the local Republican party kept my opponent in Washington for all but the last month of the campaign. That gave me a great head start. I began to relax and enjoy myself, whether I was going from door to door, from living room to living room, or from community center to community center.

Maybe I was good at campaigning because when I was a child, my family moved around a lot. Between the time I was born in Portland, Oregon, and my graduation from high school in Des Moines, Iowa, we had moved from Kansas City, Missouri, to North Platte, Nebraska, to Sioux City, Iowa, to Dallas, Texas, to Hamilton, Ohio. Starting at three, whenever we moved I had to find kids to play with in the new neighborhood, so as soon as the moving truck pulled away, I would line up my toys on the sidewalk and sit down next to them. It worked. The toys were like flypaper! I made friends almost at once.

Although I became an adept campaigner, I was so busy juggling campaign, part-time jobs, and family that I was taken by surprise when, on election day in November 1972, I won 52 percent of the vote. I wasn't expecting the victory and I certainly wasn't ready for what this would mean for me or my family. Jim wisecracked, "Well, you can't call a press conference now and say, 'I was only kidding.' "

But neither of us had a clue as to how we would uproot ourselves and resettle in Washington in two months. We were completely overwhelmed, and our way of coping was a bit unusual: we had planned—win or lose—to take the kids to Disneyland after the election, so we packed up and buzzed off to "Tomorrowland." It seemed a fitting way to start our new adventure.

A few weeks after my election, Congresswoman Bella Abzug called to congratulate me on becoming the fourteenth woman in the House of Representatives. But no sooner had she welcomed me than she asked how in the world I thought I could manage being a congresswoman and a mother with a two-year-old and a six-year-old. I told her I really wasn't sure and had hoped she would give the answer, not ask the question!

Since there was no formula written down on yellow paper, we learned by doing. There was a myriad of things to do and not much time. I made lists and my goal was to check off as many items as possible each day. We did not have time for leisurely house-hunting trips back and forth from Denver to Washington. A friend introduced us to a realtor and we gave him our minimal requirements for a house. He said, "Not much on the market between November and December. People settle in for the holidays."

One Sunday, as we were all setting forth to chop down a Christmas tree, trying to keep some semblance of normalcy for the children, the phone rang. The realtor had a house. Jim was taken to the airport to make a plane—in his tree-chopping clothes—and we got him a Big Mac to eat on the way. He was back in Denver the next day, having brought a "basic" house, period. Check off one item on the list and move on to others. In one day, over the phone, I bought two cars to move us cross-country and ordered carpeting from Denver, sight unseen, for the new house. Saving time for the family to be together became our number-one priority. Who did the wash, folded the socks, bought the groceries, or cooked the dinner became secondary. Actually, I soon learned that children don't care who does their laundry or grocery shopping or makes their beds. In fact, they don't care if anyone does it. The mystique that such tasks must be done by the hands of the mother should be buried forever so that no more guilt will be generated by it. In short order I gave up many of my ideas about what was required of a proper wife and mother.

My goal was to get the essential work done. Keeping up two households—one in Washington and one in Denver—was a matter of survival rather than gracious living.

During those first years, reporter after reporter wanted pictures and stories of the congresswoman with toddlers. They all seemed to be convinced that our family somehow wasn't normal. In a way they were right. I was the only member of Congress to come to the House floor with diapers in a handbag. Few members kept a bowl of crayons on the office coffee table or had birthday parties for their children—and a gaggle of other kindergartners— in the members' dining room. But we also lived an ordinary life in the suburbs, drove a stationwagon, and made a big deal out of holidays. It was like "Ozzie and Harriet Go to Washington."

And it was great fun. One Sunday, during the first summer we were in Washington, we were driving home from a picnic and pointing out all the tourist sites to the children. Three-year-old Jamie, looking pretty bored, asked, "When do we see Watergate?"

The kids caught on fast to their new life, as kids do. One senator I know tells the story of walking into his child's bedroom the night before they were to leave for Washington for his swearing-in. He listened as his child said his evening prayer: "God bless Mommy and Daddy and good-bye, God, tomorrow we're moving to Washington."

A few years later when Scott came home from an eight-year-old's birthday party I asked him if he'd had fun. He said, "It was okay, but parties used to be more fun when we could sing 'Happy Birthday.' " Startled, I asked him why they didn't sing it that day, and Scott explained to me that they shouldn't—until the Polish people were free.

There was a lot for all of us to learn and to cope with. From the first moment, we relied on our wits and our friends to get us through. We learned as we went along, but it wasn't always easy. Jim and I came from very different kinds of families. He was born and raised in a Chicago suburb and lived in the same house until he went to Princeton. Most of his relatives lived no more than forty miles away. Jim's mother had a master's degree and could also teach Latin, but she stayed home with her two children.

My family, on the other hand, survived on flexibility. Jim got a taste of this when, just before we were married, he came out to Iowa to spend Christmas at my parents'. The weather had turned especially cold, even for Iowa, and assuming we were going to settle in front of the fireplace, Jim began to unpack. No sooner had he begun than we made him pack his things again. My father was then in the aviation insurance business, so we went to the Des Moines Airport, rolled the family plane out of the hangar, and checked the weather briefing for pilots to decide where we could go that was warm. Jim looked puzzled by our "lack of planning." I thought all families lived like that.

In fact, I think it's the easygoing flexibility I learned from my parents that has gotten me through these hectic years. My mother worked as a schoolteacher, so when I was growing up there were days when all the balls everyone was juggling fell out of the sky at the same time. When we first married, Jim made it clear that the one thing he didn't want marriage to be was boring. Maybe he should also have said he didn't want chaos either! Ten years after we had married, settled in Denver, and begun a family, my husband had to pick up and start from scratch. Not only did moving to Washington mean he had to leave his law firm, it also cut short his own political career, which had started before mine when he ran for the state legislature in 1970 and lost by 42 votes.

We both used to tell reporters in that first year that what we desperately needed was a wife. For the first couple of months in Washington, Jim's commitments and job became secondary. Not only were we waiting for our housekeeper to come from Denver with our car, but my administrative assistant (the linchpin of any congressional office) was still in Denver and wouldn't be arriving for two months. Jim was coming with me to the Hill every day and literally couldn't get away. When an older member of Congress came by the office one day, he said to me, "I see your husband is working for you. You know you're not supposed to have him on the payroll." I answered, "Oh, he's not on the payroll. I just let him sleep with me."

Jim had thought he was set for life in a pleasant, dynamic, small Denver law firm. Then—boom!—overnight everything changed. In one way it was exciting. Not many men in their late thirties get to think seriously about whether they really like what they are doing or should contemplate a career change. In another way, my new position limited his options, so it was not as liberating as it might sound. Jim started looking for a law job as soon as life in Washington calmed down a little. But making the search more complicated was that, as the husband of a member of Congress, he had to avoid all legal work that was in any way connected with my work on the Hill. He was offered a job with the Ralph Nader organization but didn't feel it would be proper for someone who lobbied Congress to be married to one of its members. Eventually Jim's career in Washington did flourish, but getting started wasn't easy.

It wasn't easy for me either. I didn't realize before I arrived in Washington that women officeholders were considered such aberrations. The House of Representatives was not representative of the population. At that time, a growing number of women were working outside the home. But few were in Congress. Women made up a tiny minority of the House, and there were none in the Senate. I was an even bigger novelty because I was the only congresswoman with young children. In Denver, women and young voters had played a significant role in getting me elected. I hadn't realized I'd become a member of what appeared to be a College of Cardinals!

In 1973, only 27 percent of mothers who, like me, had at least one child under the age of three were in the work force. (Today that percentage has almost doubled.) I was one of the fortunate few who could afford a full-time housekeeper. Even for families with resources, housekeepers and child care were difficult to find;

for most families and for single mothers, the tighter financial bind made such help almost impossible.

Four months after I arrived in Congress I joined in a nation-wide demonstration by working mothers to protest the lack of child care in the United States and President Nixon's proposal to cut one billion dollars from forty-two social service programs. We called the protest the National Mobilization for Working Mothers. That day, women all across the country brought their kids to work with them, and my two-year-old daughter, Jamie, spent her first day in Congress. The demonstration drew a tremendous amount of criticism from conservative observers. The antipathy generated toward working women in general was harsh, but the critics reserved their worst condemnation for those who participated in the protest: these women were accused of using their innocent children to bring communism to America.

The Nixon administration wasn't new to opposing child care. My tenure as a congresswoman began in the aftermath of one of the most protracted fights on Capitol Hill, in a decade that was notorious for its political battles. In 1971, amid the clamor of the Vietnam War, Congress passed the first comprehensive child care bill. President Nixon vetoed it. This veto set the stage for a fifteen-year fight over the federal government's relationship to the American family. It colored all other policy affecting the family, from taxes to parental leave, from pension reform to abortion rights. It has taken a great many years for the shape of the debate to begin to change.

The controversy over child care has to be seen against the backdrop of the seventies. Americans were growing increasingly disturbed about our involvement in Vietnam. Women were coming together in an explosive movement to challenge sexual discrimination in the schools, the workplace, and at home. In reaction, there were many people who thought America was being turned upside down by talk about issues like the ERA, civil rights, and child care. They called the child care bill an attack by an intrusive federal government on the traditional nuclear family and even on motherhood itself. They depicted child care as a liberal plot to build huge "warehouses" for children, and to force women to leave home to go out to work. They were sure that the family was breathing its last breath.

They were wrong, of course. The American family was not in danger of extinction. Over the course of our three-hundred-year history it has weathered far-reaching social and economic change by changing dramatically itself.

The debate in the seventies was not the first time conservatives have lamented changes in the family. At the turn of the century they saw the women's suffrage movement as the beginning of the end. They thought that the increase in the number of college-educated women, many of whom were also suffragists, was responsible for rising divorce rates, decreased fertility rates, and declining morality. Universal suffrage, argued the conservatives, would be the end of the family and the end of society as we know it.

The American family survived women's suffrage and it continues to rise above the gloom-and-doom predictions of the conservatives, who, then and now, have based their criticisms on a mistaken and nostalgic view of a family that never (or hardly ever) existed. The Norman Rockwell picture that is dragged out like an icon as our ideal family is not something many Americans have experienced in real life.

Another problem is that for too long women were omitted from our history books, and only in the last twenty years has that begun to change. Yet despite a growing number of excellent books exploring women's role in American history from colonial days to the civil rights movement, women's activities and ideas have yet to become part of the common knowledge most Americans have about our past. The insinuation that women have not participated when our country needed us angers me. Patriotism and courage are not exclusively masculine traits. To think so is to ignore the contributions women have made to settling America, enriching it culturally and intellectually, and challenging it politically. Women were a major force against slavery, for expanded political rights, for good government, and for governmental involvement with the poor and dispossessed. Women have always fought alongside their husbands—and sometimes against them, as when women organized the temperance movement. And women have always worked. Women were not an idle class: they came with the first ships to Roanoke and to Plymouth, and later they picked their families up and settled the West. They worked alongside their men in the fields, and they had their own domestic responsibilities.

Too much history is focused on the "great man" idea. We all know George Washington was with his troops during the long, cold winters. But not too many people know that Martha Washington was by his side and served as nurse and cook for the troops. When the war was over, Washington made an eloquent speech before Congress to acknowledge her contribution and award her a pension for her services. Similarly, we are all familiar with the Boston Tea Party, when Massachusetts Bay colonists dressed up as Indians, made their way to British ships in the harbor, and hoisted crates of tea overboard to protest the imposition of British taxes. But there were also tea parties in South Carolina, plotted and executed by women, who were brazen enough not to wear disguises.

It's important for everyone to know that women did not sit on the sidelines and watch our country's history unfold. We pitched in and made history, too. In 1979, I sponsored the Minutewomen Series, opening every legislative day in the House during July with a one-minute speech about women's contributions to American history. Obviously, twenty minutes was not enough time to fully explain American women's contributions, but it was long enough to spark the interest of men and women all across America. A teacher from Michigan wrote me that she made copies of all the speeches and used them as a text for her seventh-grade social studies class.

If women remain ignorant of their role in history, they may be reluctant to participate in debates that will dictate the future of their children and their country. Women can take courage from the achievement of those who came before them.

The idea that women did not have an important role to play seemed foreign to me for personal reasons as well. The women around me when I was growing up all worked. My mother was a schoolteacher and returned to the classroom as soon as I started kindergarten. I don't think my family was unusual: women have always worked, in circumstances that varied with class and geography. Poor and immigrant women either worked outside the home or took in work. Almost all women did housework. Women who could hire housekeepers very often did volunteer work. They may not have been salaried but they worked.

The view of men as breadwinners and women as wives and mothers continues to have a strong hold on some policymakers, educators, and corporate executives. It is mirrored in legislative policy that puts women at a disadvantage, discriminates against them in the workplace, and undermines their economic security. Many people today, as in the past, fight legislation that would acknowledge the kinds of lives women really lead, for fear they'll be accused of destroying the mythical family. I think we need to take back the traditional definition of the family as an economic unit and basic building block of our society and get on with reinforcing it.

By the time I reached Congress, what I knew or thought I knew from experience about the American family was showing up in statistics. Although women still earned less than men, even if they did the same job, the number of working women continued to grow. In the boom economy of the postwar years, anything seemed possible. The American dream of owning a car and a house and sending the children to college had become a reality for more and more Americans. Wages rose during the fifties and sixties and the economy expanded; but with the recessions of the early seventies, for many families, the woman's salary had become essential if the children were to go to college or the mortgage was to get paid. The combination of economic stagnation and inflation was pulling more and more women into the work force. The economy did more to put women in the workplace than feminism did or, certainly, than progressive legislation did.

Something else was going on, too. With the growth of the women's movement, the strict definition of what women could do was changing. In my own family, my father had encouraged me to become a lawyer. He never hesitated to stand behind me when I wanted to do something unconventional. I learned to fly by the time I was fifteen and I was encouraged to be an independent thinker. But, even so, both he and my mom were unsure that Harvard was the right law school for me. They were concerned more about my being one of a handful of women in a school that had only recently accepted female students than about whether I could make it academically. They worried also that no one would want to marry me if I had a law degree. "You're nobody until you're Mrs. Somebody" was believed even by my progressive parents. During those Harvard years, when people asked my mother where I was, she'd say, "Oh, back East. On some project." She was afraid that if word got out that I was at Harvard Law, I'd never get a husband and she'd never be a grandmother! (Of course I fooled her by marrying another law student.)

When I got to Harvard, I found myself submerged in sexism. On my first day, one of my male classmates refused to take his assigned seat when he saw that he had been placed next to a woman—next to me, that is. He let me know that he had never gone to school with a girl before and he didn't think he should have to start now. Before he stomped off to have his seat changed, he also sniped that I should be ashamed of myself for taking up a spot in the class that should have gone to a man. "Sexagrated" schools were prevalent then, and a high percentage of the members of the class had been in single-sex schools all their lives.

I rarely hear that kind of overt sexism today. When I recently returned to Harvard to give a speech, I realized how many of the barriers women faced in the past have broken down. The number of women law students almost equals that of male students. Women have made inroads into practically every profession. No one would stop to question a coed today about going to graduate school. Yet when she graduates, we make it extremely hard for her to practice her profession if she decides to have not only a career but a family as well. Women today face new barriers based on the same old stereotypes. Whether I speak to women physicians or psychologists, women business executives or telephone operators, women carpenters or nurses, I find they all face a common problem: most employers either ignore their employees' responsibilities to their families or overemphasize them and use the family as an excuse to deny promotion.

Government and employment policies lag far behind the realities faced by today's working families. In the seventies women were told, "Okay, if you think you can be supermom, then what you have to do is look like a *Vogue* model, be a great wife, bake cookies for your kids every day, iron your husband's handkerchiefs, and work at your job and in the home about eighty hours a week. Go for it!" People who talked like this thought they had heard women saying they were superior, when in fact they were only saying they were equal. When women collapsed of exhaustion, these same folks wrote books saying, "See? Women aren't superior after all."

I did not come to Washington only to champion women's rights and the American family. I thought of myself as one of the many men and women across the country who were working together to improve the quality of life on many fronts. Gloria Steinem helped me raise money for my 1972 race and for subsequent campaigns, and I belonged to and participated in several women's groups. But I knew that there were many areas of American life the government had neglected, not only the so-called women's issues. Yet if I wanted money for education, for cleaning up the environment, or for anything else, I would be told, "Great idea, Pat, but no money. There are always more good ideas than there is money, Pat. You'll learn this when you've been in Washington longer."

That kind of talk, as well as my interest in ending the Vietnam War, made me decide to get on the committee where the most discretionary money is spent: Armed Services. My first fight in Congress therefore was a very tough one, for the committee was then a male bastion.

Being a liberal freshman woman made me a long shot for the slot. It also didn't help that the chairman of the committee, F. Edward Hebert, a conservative Southern Democrat who boasted about his male chauvinism, did not consider me worthy of the seat. Women, he claimed, knew nothing of combat, since historically they had never been a part of it. His reasoning seemed to me to be completely bogus, since many of the male committee members, in spite of their rhetoric, had never served in the armed forces either. I studied the war records of all the committee members, and when those who had never served in the armed forces tried to embarrass me by asking, "How can you serve on this committee? You have never been in combat," I would calmly reply, "Then you and I have a lot in common."

From what I had observed, it seemed to me the committee often justified its actions in the name of defending women and children and yet it never bothered to ask women and children what they wanted. I finally succeeded in getting a place on the Armed Services Committee against the wishes of the chairman, but not without the kind of battle few of my male colleagues had to wage in their first few days in the Capitol. By comparison, my first day at Harvard seemed like a welcoming party.

My congressional interests were broad, but pushing women's equality has always been important to me. I am constantly surprised by women who, when elected, immediately say, "I am not 'just' a woman." What a self-image! From my earliest days in Congress I noticed that many women, visiting Washington, would stop to see the representative of their home district and

then come by to see me, their "congresswoman." These meetings, and the letters I got, all began the same way—with a short
apology, because the woman was not from my district, and then
the explanation that she didn't know where else to go. The letters
and visits had a common complaint: the people who made laws
were out of touch.

Among those who contacted me might be a daughter caring for
aging parents; or a new mother wanting to return to work; or a
former wife who wasn't eligible for any of the pension of a
divorced husband; or a young single mother who couldn't get
time off to be with her seriously ill child. Some of the women I
heard from wanted advice about when was a good time to have
a baby, or what employers offered flexitime programs, job-shar-
ing, or part-time jobs with adequate benefits, so they could spend
more time with their children and continue to work.

My work in Congress has been largely to counter the conservative policy of retreating to a romanticized past. Conservatives
have fought against removing the barriers women encountered in
the universities and the workplace. They have fought enlightened
social policy and thus have added to the tremendous stress families are under. Luckily, most people, including many policymakers, are beginning to recognize the real changes that have taken
place in the modern family; what has not yet happened is a
general acknowledgment that the family's needs have changed as
well, and that we need new policies that address those needs.
Women and men do not stop being parents at the office door or
the factory gate. They require a responsive workplace and a
sensitive legislature to help them meet their responsibilities.
Many women leaders of the conservative movement have run
through every door opened for women, never said thanks, fought
furiously against the opening of further doors, but then have run
through the newly opened doors as fast as they could. Out West
we'd call that rude and hypocritical!

The issues struck a personal chord for me. From the moment
I won my first congressional campaign I had a gnawing feeling

that this might be one job I couldn't do. In an attempt to quell my panic, my rational side, what I think of as the lawyer side of me, pooh-poohed my doubts and drew up—as any good lawyer would—a list of my accomplishments. But it didn't always work. I found, to my surprise, that my fears echoed the common mythology that a woman couldn't be a member of Congress and especially that a mother couldn't and shouldn't combine career and family. Despite my education and the changing times, I had to disprove these myths for myself. I learned to overcome them, but I thank goodness my daughter will not have the same doubts. I hope she will also have fewer of the problems.

3

The Serious Matter
of Motherhood

"I have a uterus and a brain and they both work"—this was the answer I gave once, after being asked over and over, "How can you be both a mother and a congresswoman?" I try to engage my brain before opening my mouth but sometimes my impatience wins.

I have been asked many times what I consider my greatest achievement. With no hesitation, I always reply, "Scott and Jamie, my two children."

From the time I was a little girl I never questioned whether or not I would have children. I wanted a family like the one I grew up in. We were a tight-knit group of four—Mom, Dad, my brother, Mike, and I. The family was a team that worked together. Because my mother was a public school teacher, we treated the whole house like a bulletin board, especially on holidays. We'd hang pictures of turkeys on Thanksgiving and home-made decorations on Christmas, and on Washington's Birthday, we painted grapefruits red to look like cherries—sort of swollen cherries.

Dad was a resourceful man who valued time so much that he would mow the grass in his suit because he didn't want to waste time changing clothes. He hated to see his children idle and encouraged us to take up various projects. I learned to fly and Mike rebuilt cars, and when we had a spare moment we were expected to help Dad with his projects—rebuilding an airplane or remodeling a house. He even suggested to boys I was dating in high school that they come over and work on the house instead of going out to the movies with me. Nice, Dad!

When Jim and I married, I just assumed we'd have no trouble having children. Wrong! My body did not respond to my commands, and I discovered that pregnancy could be life-threatening for me and my babies. I have been pregnant three times and each time was traumatic.

In 1966, four years after we were married, I was pregnant with Scott. I thought I was so smart! I'd finished law school and had worked for two years, so it was now a "convenient" time to have a baby. For the first three months of the pregnancy my only problem was the normal morning nausea, and I even loved that, for finally I had a reason to eat crackers in bed before I got up!

We bought a brand-new contemporary A-frame house in Colorado. The builder had gone bankrupt, so we got it at a great price. We loved our living room with its soaring forty-foot ceiling and the master bedroom on a balcony overlooking the living room. The only trouble was that several times I'd come home from work and smelled gas. I'd call the repairmen; they'd look at the furnace and say that nothing was wrong.

I thought no more about it until one night when we had a dinner party for friends. One couple was a doctor and a nurse, the other a dentist and a dental hygienist. By nine-thirty, all our guests were so tired they left. That was highly unusual, but we ourselves were so exhausted we didn't protest and just dropped into bed. I got up several times during the night, feeling nauseated, but attributed this to my pregnancy. Once, however, I was awakened by a great racket. I stumbled to the balcony, looked over, and saw Jim lying flat on the floor with his head bleeding. My own head felt very fuzzy. I went downstairs and struggled to open the door to the outside. A neighbor's beagle, named Tom Dooley, ran in and started licking Jim's head. The neighbor, seeing the door ajar, followed him and smelled the gas immediately. He got us outside and called an ambulance. The doctor sewed Jim up and told us we were very fortunate, for most people would just have slept away, never to wake.

During the night, Jim had finally realized that something was wrong, but by then he was not thinking clearly. His solution had been to try to turn off the thermostat with a fireplace tool. Then he fell on the tool and cut his head.

As it turned out, there was nothing wrong with the furnace itself. The exhaust had not been installed properly and when the wind blew from a certain direction, the carbon monoxide backed into the house. The A-frame created a vacuum effect under those rare wind conditions. Great!

Some nerve endings on Jim's head died as a result of his injury and for about a year he had patches of baldness. For six months, though, we were terribly worried about the effects of the gas on the baby. I think every parent has doubts and fears during pregnancy, but mine were almost obsessive. It was as if headlines kept running through my head, as they do on Times Square in New York: WILL HE BE PHYSICALLY DEFORMED? WILL HE BE MENTALLY RETARDED? The doctors played straight with me and said they didn't know. I went into labor six weeks early, and as the doctor looked at the baby, he asked me for the name of my neurosurgeon. He thought that Scott's head was larger than normal and that he might be hydrocephalic. He was right to be cautious, but for the next several months, I had to keep taking the baby to the doctor to get his head measured. It wasn't until Scott was six months old that he was finally given a clean bill of health and Jim and I could breathe a sigh of relief. During that anxious time we had dug out old baby books of everyone in the family to do comparisons of head sizes. It turns out there are big heads on both sides of the family, so for us, Scott was just normal.

I was not apprehensive about having more children because I thought the odds against another freak furnace accident were a million to one! Two years later I became pregnant again, and this time I expected everything to be easy. I was especially thrilled because my brother, Mike, and his wife, Julie, were also going to have a baby. But during the fourth month, something was clearly going wrong. My obstetrician explained that I was bleeding because I was "high-strung." On it went for months—I would complain about the bleeding, he would say the problem was all in my head, that being a Harvard lawyer, I was just having trouble adjusting to life as a housewife! I was so weak I couldn't argue. (Believe me, that is weak!) Then, several weeks later, I was horrified when my sister-in-law, Julie, lost her baby. I began to worry more about mine. A month later, eight weeks before I was due, I went into labor and was rushed to the hospital. We checked in and then discovered that no one could find the doctor. For twelve hours I waited in a small room, buzzing the nurse from time to time to ask whether another doctor could look at me because I knew there was something terribly wrong. The nurse (who repeatedly claimed she went to high school with me) kept telling me to calm down. She said over and over again that nothing was wrong and that there were plenty of women just like me having babies in the hospital. I would have to wait my turn. Grow up. Her condescending manner was infuriating. Jim was home with Scott and a houseful of weekend guests. The nurses wouldn't let me near a phone. Obviously the doctors were also enjoying their weekends and didn't want to be bothered. No nurse wanted to risk being shouted at by a doctor for "overreacting." The whole incident was a nightmare, and I hope I never again feel as alone and helpless as I did that day in one of America's most modern hospitals.

My doctor eventually arrived and the delivery proceeded. He immediately said, "Something is terribly wrong." He discovered I had twins—a boy and a girl. All he could say was "Oh, my God, we should have done a cesarean." The girl had died earlier in the pregnancy and this had been the cause of my hemorrhaging. She was born first and it was very difficult. The boy was alive, but barely, weighing only four and a half pounds. The delivery was very hard on him. We tried, with no luck, to get him into a hospital that had equipment to keep him alive. He died the next morning of a brain hemorrhage caused by the pressure of a difficult delivery. The hospital authorities put me in a room with other women who had given birth to healthy children. They were torn apart, wanting to enjoy their babies but feeling terrible about me. I couldn't stand the situation and so I sneaked out of the hospital and went home. I never wanted to see the place again.

This second pregnancy had been an intense, draining, and humiliating nightmare. I was angry at the doctor for his refusal to listen to me. I was angry at the hospital and the nurse for the same reason. But most of all, I was angry at myself for having put up with it all. Here I was, a trained lawyer, letting a doctor convince me I had no right to question his judgment about *my* pregnancy and *my* baby. He intimidated me and made me feel powerless. It worked. I didn't speak out. The hospital staff also put me in a position of surrendering all control to them. Never again. I decided to act on my anger. The next month, I shopped around for a new doctor. I made appointments and asked questions of as many doctors as I could, until I met one I could trust and who treated me like a thinking human being. Changing doctors made a difference. My next pregnancy, in 1970, with my daughter, Jamie, was a pleasant nine months. Finally!

But although my pregnancy was normal, it also almost killed me. Jamie and I had been home from the hospital two days when I started hemorrhaging. No one could stop it. Jim, who had been campaigning for a Colorado State House seat, rushed me to the hospital, where death courted me for six weeks. I spent my thirtieth birthday in intensive care, floating in and out of consciousness, certain I was going to die. Meanwhile, Jim was at home with a four-year-old child and a two-week-old baby, trying to care for them, visit me, keep up with his job, and run for office. When I finally recovered, the doctors warned me, "We don't want to see you here again. Another baby could kill you."

These experiences certainly reinforced my belief that a woman has a right to decide what happens to her own body. That is a basic right, and it should not be curtailed by the government or anyone else. There was no doubt in my mind that I should not get pregnant again. Pregnancy is not like a nine-month cruise; it can be life-threatening. I also understood that other women may have compelling reasons to avoid a pregnancy that could wreak havoc with their lives and the lives of their children. For this reason, I was active on reproductive health issues long before I became politically active. I have always been amazed that a fetus is assigned a personality immediately upon conception—girls have hair ribbons and are holding dolls in the womb, boys are playing with trucks—but the woman is rarely mentioned by conservatives in debates on reproduction. She is just an impersonal receptor. She has no right to decide what is best for herself or any children she might have. This kind of thinking seems illogical and insane to me.

Family planning was very controversial when I was at Harvard. In 1962, the first year Jim and I were married, contraceptives were illegal in Massachusetts. Though I could get prescriptions for birth control pills at the student clinic, I would have to wait until we visited my folks in Iowa or Jim's folks in Illinois to have the prescriptions filled. Three years later, in 1965, the Supreme Court ruled in *Griswold v. Connecticut* that married couples throughout the country had the right to obtain contraceptives. This ruling overrode state laws preventing such access and paved the way for contraception to become legal and accepted. After law school, when Jim and I moved to Denver, I volunteered and did pro bono legal work for the Rocky Mountain Planned Parenthood organization until I was elected to Congress.

On January 22, 1973, during my first month as a congresswoman, the Supreme Court handed down a decision on a woman's right to choose whether or not to have a baby. *Roe v. Wade* dramatically changed the scale of the controversy over birth control. It made a woman's right to an abortion the law of the land and virtually eliminated illegal abortions, with their alarmingly high mortality rates. Even though, prior to the ruling, seventeen states had adopted laws making certain abortions legal, and nearly 600,000 women had obtained legal abortions in 1972, the Center for Disease Control estimates that another 130,000 women had to resort to illegal or self-induced procedures.[1]

Roe v. Wade sparked a fervent nationwide debate that has not faded to this day. Despite what the critics say, I am pro-life *as well as* pro-choice. Obviously I wanted a family—I had to struggle hard to have babies, and my children are the source of my own strength. But I feel that every woman has to make her own decision about family size, depending on her circumstances, religious beliefs, and medical advice. To have an abortion is very difficult. Women do not take this step lightly. But their right to this choice is a fundamental liberty. I always bristle when people argue that women want abortion mainly as a form of birth control. I certainly think there are forms of birth control that are a lot easier.

Anti-family-planning and anti-abortion organizations sprang up in the wake of *Roe v. Wade,* armed with proposed constitutional amendments and legislation to outlaw contraceptives and abortions. Abortion became a moral battlefield on which conservatives and liberals fought out the definition of women's role in society. Both sides understood that the Supreme Court decision was as much about an individual woman's right to determine what happened to her own body as it was about abortion. With the legal authority to make decisions about childbearing, women gained power over their own lives.

One reason the debate became so volatile was that right-to-life organizations were extremely graphic in their depiction of abortion. They would, for example, deluge congressional offices with postcards of aborted fetuses, not bothering to say that most of the pictures showed fetuses from pregnancies that were further along than most pregnancies at the time of abortion. They made misleading films and created slogans out of hard questions. They were able to portray abortion as an absolute issue. They ignored the women, and their families, and the complex reasons for their choices.

I worked with the National Abortion Rights Action League (NARAL) to bring to Washington personal stories from women who chose abortion in tragic circumstances. I then asked members of Congress to read letters from such women during a congressional session. The stories were extremely moving, and it's hard to imagine what kind of person would not respond to them. One was from a woman whose aunt had died from a back-alley abortion, another from a young teenager who said she felt she had only two choices before her—abortion or suicide. These brave women came forward with their experiences to illustrate how difficult a choice abortion is. They reminded us that there are two lives involved in an abortion. I don't think it is within my power as a lawmaker to decide which life has the greater right to exist.

Unfortunately, neither these stories nor opinion polls showing strong public support for a woman's right to abortion have overcome the strength of the right-to-life movement when it comes to influencing Congress. These groups have been able to prohibit government funding of abortions and add anti-abortion restrictions to legislation. Over the years, they have curtailed the abortion rights of forty million Americans, including low-income women, federal employees, military personnel, retirees and their dependents, American Indian women, Peace Corps volunteers, and teenage girls. I wish that instead they would join me in supporting research to find a safe and totally effective contraceptive so the question of abortion would be moot.

In Congress, I have opposed limiting abortion rights, but as much as I support a woman's right to choice, I must reemphasize that I think abortion is a terrible form of birth control. I would like to see the right-to-life organizations work with pro-choice organizations to inform people, especially our young sons and daughters, about how to prevent pregnancy. I think it would be great if we could get teenagers to abstain from sex altogether until

they are out of high school. However, making virginity a graduation requirement won't do it. The need for responsible sexual
behavior must be communicated to our kids. The fact is that
sexual activity among teens is increasing, and the United States
has the highest teenage pregnancy rate of any developed country
in the Western world.[2]

The solutions some conservatives have recommended are almost laughable. They have even asked for federal money to set
up chastity clinics. It seems to me the federal government knows
nothing about the subject, certainly not enough to teach it. Also,
given what the statistics show about teenagers, it is very unrealis-
tic to think they are going to flock to these centers to absorb
moralistic pearls of wisdom from the feds: wouldn't you love to
know what kind of teenage years the proponents of such clinics
had?

On the other hand, I think it would be useful if communities
would sponsor forums where foreign students and American
students who have lived abroad could share their knowledge of
how other countries deal with teenage sexuality. Listening to
teens who have lived in other cultures can be very informative.

Teen pregnancy isn't a new problem. Though making abortions available to young people has somewhat lowered the birth
rate, a great many babies are still being born to teenagers, most
of them unmarried girls under the age of eighteen. The personal
and social costs to these new parents are staggering. And we have
only begun to feel the cost to society. On economic grounds
alone, it is hard to see how we will be able to care for and educate
these children in generations to come. So many of the most rabid
right-to-lifers don't address this question. They seem to believe
life begins at conception and ends at birth. The teen and baby are
on their own after the birth.

Curbing teenage pregnancy is not simple. Education is clearly
one factor. We have practically no comprehensive sex education
in our schools in this country. We must have it. But we should

combine information on contraception with lessons on family values, sexual responsibility, and respect for one another. The National Research Council issued a report for 1987 that pointed out the connection between teens' sexual activity, including their use of birth control, and their perceptions of their lives and their future. The brighter they saw their future, the more likely they were to be sexually responsible.[3]

Our challenge is to make being pregnant "uncool" for teenagers. This task is made especially difficult by our culture. Americans are bombarded with messages of sexuality from television, pop music, movies, and magazines. Teens are aware that glamorous unwed movie stars have babies. They constantly see sexual relationships on TV. But they don't see the consequences—the strain of pregnancy and new parenthood on young lives, or the lingering and sometimes fatal effects of sexually transmitted disease.

The effort to challenge peer pressure to have sex, and even to have babies, has to involve parents as well as teenagers. In order for teens to practice responsible sexual behavior, they need information. The way it is now, when kids try to learn about birth control, we place obstacles in front of them. The "squeal rule," a regulation that parents must be notified before a teenager is given contraceptives, presents such an obstacle. So does the recent Supreme Court ruling that gave schools the right to censor school newspapers, in this case, articles written on teen pregnancy and on divorce. Parents need to understand that giving young people information about sex does not encourage them to have sex. It encourages them to act responsibly. Teens want us to deal straight with them. Unless we give them the facts, we stand on shaky ground when we complain about their actions. We often treat our children as if they were hothouse plants. They aren't, and since they don't lead sheltered lives, they must make hard choices. We should prepare them.

When I have visited programs for teen mothers in schools and young women's residences, the girls consistently tell me two things: first, they didn't realize what a responsibility motherhood would be; second, they have learned that education is the key to improving their lives and those of their babies. A Boston doctor told me that she had seen many young girls give up their babies after a couple of weeks because they were so overwhelmed by the responsibility of caring for them. They weren't ready. Babies don't come with directions written on the back or batteries that can be removed. Motherhood is twenty-four hours a day, seven days a week. You can't "leave the office." Teenagers are too young to be ready. We should help them understand that *before* they get pregnant.

In 1988, I toured a residence for young women in Florida with my friend Dr. T. Berry Brazelton, the Harvard pediatrician. At first the girls were wary, but after Dr. Brazelton talked about being ready for motherhood and the need to teach people how to be parents, our audience warmed up. They understood. They were living with the problems he was discussing.

Teen pregnancy is as much a product of economic conditions as it is of misinformation and cultural influences. Statistics show that teen parents are more likely than other teens to come from poor families. Further, they are more apt to drop out of school, thus passing on the sad legacy of poverty to another generation. The Children's Defense Fund found that young women who were poor and had below-average academic skills were five and a half times more likely than other teenage girls to become teen parents.

Teenage boys and girls need the education and training necessary to prepare them for decent jobs so that they can break out of the pattern of poverty and early parenthood. Black teenage boys have the highest unemployment rate in the country. The truth of the matter is that there are very few jobs available to them. We have to focus on efforts to turn that situation around. We are stripping their masculinity away, for these young men see no hope of providing for a family.

In addition, for young girls, we need to redouble our efforts to keep abortions safe and legal. We must make sure that those young girls and women who depend on federal assistance have the same reproductive health rights and access to information and services as middle-class and upper-class women do. However, we must emphasize that informed, sensible, and responsible behavior, not abortion, is the best form of birth control. Finally, overseas, our birth control programs have been reduced to teaching one method only: the rhythm system. This ridiculous legacy of the Reagan years must be reversed.

Just as public policy should provide options for people who want to limit their family size, it should also extend choices to those who want to have a family but can't. Infertility and the new reproductive technologies will be important family health issues of the twenty-first century. Infertility strikes at least one in five American couples, yet it is overlooked as a serious problem and ignored as a legitimate health issue. Insurance companies often deem it extraneous to health care, the press portrays it as a "yuppie" problem, and much of the public still believes all you have to do to have babies is relax. The number of couples unable to conceive a baby is increasing. The infertility rate among married women twenty to twenty-four years old has tripled in the past twenty years. And infertility is not just a women's problem; it occurs as frequently in men.[4]

There are many reasons why some couples can't easily produce children. Age is one of them. Some women who wait until they are financially secure and emotionally prepared to have a family may be less fertile than they were when younger; such women are victims of their own biological clocks. The rise of sexually transmitted diseases that can damage the reproductive system is another factor. I also think environmental problems will eventually be shown to have a large effect on our increasing infertility problem.

When you want children, the inability to have them comes as

a terrible surprise. I have been moved by the stories of infertile couples who have testified before me at hearings. They have shown inspiring stamina and determination, spending months and sometimes years going through seemingly endless tests and treatments, never certain whether the latest procedure would work. Along the way they experience disappointment, anger, pain, embarrassment, and desperation. One man told me that during his three years of treatment, he and his wife were "paralyzed by sadness." Yet for them, the possibility that they might one day be able to have children of their own made the emotional ups and downs worthwhile.

The good news is that the medical world has made significant advances in the treatment of infertility. New drugs, artificial insemination, and in vitro fertilization (IVF) are now much more widely available. Through modern technology, doctors can now diagnose and treat over half of those with infertility problems. The bad news is that many childless couples cannot afford to pursue either the diagnosis or the cure. While the cost of treatment should average around $3,000, several couples have written me that their expenses ran up to $50,000. IVF alone, while usually the procedure of last resort, costs between $3,500 and $6,000 per treatment. One couple told me of the trauma of selling their house to pay for two in vitro fertilization treatments. The procedures didn't work; now they have neither a house or a baby.[5]

Just as the cost of pregnancy and delivery should not discourage people from pursuing their commitment to parenthood, the expense of treating infertility should not place children beyond the reach of prospective parents. Health insurance makes it possible for most couples to afford to have a family, but not the infertile couple. Their effort to have a child is at great personal expense, with no guarantee of success.

Prices for fertility treatments may be high when shouldered by individuals, but they would add little (approximately one tenth of one percent) to the nation's health care bill if covered by insurance.[6] As chairwoman of the Civil Service Subcommittee, I proposed legislation requiring the companies insuring federal workers to cover the costs of infertility treatments. Although the legislation is limited to the federal work force, my hope is that it will serve as a model for private employers to provide comprehensive benefits for their workers. Insurers object because they claim that fertility treatments are not health-related; yet they cover vasectomies and tubal ligation. They also say that such treatments are too costly, but cost is not a good reason for such discrimination. Moreover, we found from the experience of states that have already passed laws mandating coverage by insurance companies dealing with the private sector (Massachusetts, Texas, Hawaii, Arkansas, and Maryland) that costs for fertility treatment are far lower than what was projected.

Another option for childless couples is adoption. But it, too, is a long, costly, and uncertain process. Many adoption agencies have requirements concerning a couple's age, their religion, and their financial status. If accepted, the couple must go through another waiting period, anywhere from one month to five or six years. Often there is little advance notice before a baby becomes available. When a child is found, the couple must immediately come up with a large sum of money. For example, average adoption costs for a child run between $5,000 and $10,000. These expenses are not tax deductible and are not covered by insurance. According to the National Committee for Adoption, many would-be adoptive parents, especially minority parents, are simply denied the adoption alternative because they lack the money. A woman testified eloquently before the House Post Office and Civil Service Committee that to adopt her Vietnamese son, she had to pay more than $10,000. Her family's income was under $25,000 per year.[7]

My legislation to have insurance companies cover infertility treatments would also have them cover the costs of adoption. To come up with this proposal, I have worked with an unlikely ally,

Sen. Gordon Humphrey of New Hampshire, one of the most outspoken advocates in Congress for the right-to-life organizations. In 1987 we were able to pass into law a two-year test program to reimburse members of the military, whose efforts to adopt are further complicated by the military's frequent tour-of-duty moves and low pay. I have also advocated allowing adoptive parents to take tax deductions for the expenses of the adoption process. We allow tax relief for breeding thoroughbred horses, why not for adopting children?

Adoptions are, for the most part, a matter of state jurisdiction, but national policymakers can take steps to make adoption more accessible. Many working couples who want to adopt a child cannot do so because of the usual requirement that one parent must be at home with the child for at least the first six months. For many people, this means choosing between their dream of a family and their need for a job. The proposed Family and Medical Leave Act allows all working parents, including those who adopt, to take an unpaid leave from their jobs so that they can bond with their new child and begin the process of becoming a family.

Government should not be our nanny. We should not become dependent on the government to sustain us. But neither should politicians dictate how we live our private lives or interfere in our most private decisions. Our government has a responsibility, one that other governments in the free world have accepted, to come up with options that will help those who want to have families as well as those who don't.

Government should encourage research and development of new technology to help couples who are fertile as well as those who are infertile. Government also has a responsibility to educate the public about issues related to childbearing. People need to know how they can treat infertility or prevent pregnancy. Pregnant women need to know the importance of good prenatal care. This country has one of the highest infant mortality rates in the industrialized world, primarily because mothers cannot afford good prenatal care.

Empowerment involves the combination of knowledge and resources. Government policy in both these is now left to chance. That is shameful.

4

Parental Leave

FOR the first time in our history the majority of American women in their childbearing years are also working outside the home. The decision to start a family or have another child is no longer simply a private one between husband and wife; it also involves their bosses. An expectant mother must consider whether she can take leave to have her baby; whether the leave will be paid; whether she will continue to receive health insurance; and, most important, whether there will be a job for her when she is ready to go back to work.

Quite understandably, women are very concerned about these matters. All across the country they ask me, "When is the best time to have a baby?" At first they used to pull me aside and question me privately, after I had given a speech. Now, more and more, they are asking publicly during the formal question-and-answer period—regardless of what the speech is about. Even college-age women who have not yet embarked on their careers ask the same question.

At first, I was a little taken aback. I thought, How can I answer such a personal question? Soon I realized that their concern was an individual one—"How in the world am I going to do it all?—as well as a collective plea for help to bring about changes in employment policies to accommodate parents juggling work and kids.

In my own life, it was deciding to get married that was the big step. Jim and I laugh about the money that changed hands on the steps of the church the day we got married. We spent hours and days together pondering what our marriage would mean. I knew that the one thing I didn't want was a sequestered existence in the suburbs. I grew up thinking anything was possible—flying airplanes, going to Harvard—and I wanted to make sure my marriage would have the same kind of open atmosphere. I always preferred having wings to having things. Thank goodness, Jim understood and agreed.

My ideas were a little more conventional when it came time to start a family. I was working full-time as a field attorney at the National Labor Relations Board in Denver, and I didn't even bother to find out whether the NLRB had a maternity-leave policy. In 1966, the prevailing policy was "You get pregnant, you leave." If I had asked about taking maternity leave, my employers would have laughed. Soon after becoming pregnant I made plans to leave the board and stay at home as a full-time mother. That is what my mother had done, and I took it for granted that I should too. Economics did not play a part in my decision because, like many young couples at the time (and unlike the situation today), we were able to get by on one income. I also felt, and still do, that it is good if you can manage to be with a child the first few months after it is born.

When I was expecting my first child, it was commonly believed that a woman about to have a child didn't belong in the workplace. Pregnancy was treated as a "condition" that required special protection. In practice, employees who did not quit after they became pregnant were asked to take leave from their jobs. In the public schools where my mother had taught, teachers had to leave their jobs before they began to "show." During my own pregnancy, I had to try a case before a sixty-year-old hearing officer who was a bachelor. He was panicked by my "condition," and kept asking me if I wanted to sit down, eat, excuse myself. It was more like a Peter Sellers movie than a Perry Mason show.

Private employers at the time didn't do better. General Electric, like most businesses, required its pregnant employees to take leave three months prior to giving birth, without any compensation or disability benefits. A woman's desire to work or her physical ability to do so didn't matter. Employers did not consider women a permanent part of the work force. To be fair, in part, this was true. When I quit the NLRB, only about 25 percent of the women who left work to have a baby returned to work within twelve months. But what employers failed to recognize was that even then, the majority of these mothers would return to work when their children began school.

Popular attitudes about pregnancy have come a long way since I had my children, and the women's movement has had a lot to do with it. But the change in attitude did not come easily. It was not until 1984 that the American Medical Association admitted that its previous recommendation on pregnancy and work—that a woman should stop working in her sixth month—was based more on myth than on science.

The federal government has also been slow to respond to the problem. For example, during Franklin Roosevelt's administration in World War II, the work force was increasingly composed of women. Under the direction of Frances Perkins, then Secretary of Labor and the first woman to hold a Cabinet position, the Women's Bureau issued guidelines calling for job-protected leaves for pregnant women. Noting that "some women who are pregnant or who have young children may find it necessary to work," the bureau made some enlightened recommendations: a limited workday, rest periods, six weeks of prenatal leave, and two months of postnatal leave.[1] These were the suggestions. In practice, very little was done.

Two decades later, the federal government again turned its attention to pregnant women. In 1963, the President's Commission on the Status of Women set up two task forces to look specifically at the problem of maternity benefits for working women. The commission recommended that employers, unions, and the government explore means of providing a paid maternity leave or comparable insurance benefits for at least six months, without reemployment being forfeited. But the recommendations did not find their way into legislation and were once again forgotten.

Finally, in 1964, Congress passed the Civil Rights Act, prohibiting discrimination on the basis of race, religion, national origin, or sex. The law was as significant a turning point for women as it was for blacks and other minorities. The word "sex" was added as a last-minute ploy by one Southern conservative to kill the civil rights bill altogether. But once it was included, members fought hard to keep protection for women in the bill. Proponents believed that, among other benefits, the law would extend protection to pregnant workers.

Wrong. That made too much sense. The Equal Employment Opportunity Commission (EEOC), charged with implementation, flip-flopped on the issue of whether pregnancy fell within the reach of the law. At first the commission said it didn't and then, in 1972, it reversed itself, telling employers to treat pregnancy as they did other disabilities. The confusion found its way into the courts. While the debate was going on, women were forced to take maternity leave, they got fired, *and* they were denied disability and maternity benefits.

By 1976 things came to a head. The Supreme Court agreed to hear the case of *General Electric Co. v. Gilbert* (429 U.S. 125), to decide whether GE had discriminated against its female employees by excluding pregnancy from coverage under its disability plan. The Court's decision would set the standard for the entire country. To my utter surprise, the Supreme Court, reversing the decisions of seven federal courts of appeal and numerous lower federal courts throughout the country, found that discriminating against pregnancy does not constitute sex discrimination. They held that pregnancy is not a sex-related condition! Had any members of the then entirely male Court been pregnant?

The decision sent shock waves through the country. Comics

loved it. It seemed incredible that the highest court in the land would rule that to treat pregnancy-related disabilities differently from other temporary disabilities was not sex discrimination. Like me, many of my colleagues in the House and Senate believed that the Court had ignored the intent of Congress in its interpretation of the Civil Rights Act. We were outraged. The Court's reasoning was that no pregnant *person* would be covered—pregnancy as a condition was the issue, not gender. Through some Alice-in-Wonderland logic the Court convinced itself it was being absolutely evenhanded. After all, if men got pregnant, they too would be denied these benefits. To make matters worse, part of the Court's thinking rested on the premise that pregnancy was a "voluntary" condition and therefore did not have to be included in a disability benefit package. But GE's disability plan covered voluntary conditions like sports injuries, attempted suicides, venereal disease, disabilities incurred in the commission of a crime or during a fight, and vasectomies. The only voluntary activity not covered was procreation.

I told one reporter that the logic reminded me of a Canadian case that had been a favorite of mine during law school. As I remember, the case went something like this: An Indian using bow and arrow shot a horse wearing a feather blanket. There was no law on the books against shooting a horse with an arrow, but there was one against shooting migratory birds. So the court found the horse was really a migratory bird and upheld the conviction of the arrow-wielder.

The Court's decision aroused Congress to action. On March 15, 1977, I joined with eighty-one of my colleagues to introduce the Pregnancy Discrimination Act to amend the Civil Rights Act of 1964 so that it would specifically include pregnancy. Over forty women's organizations, civil rights groups, and labor unions formed the Campaign to End Discrimination Against Pregnant Workers. In 1978 the Pregnancy Discrimination Act (PDA) became law, with the result that pregnancy had to be treated like any other temporary disability. But the law did not direct employers to reinstate women in their jobs after they recovered from childbirth, nor did it provide them with disability benefits other than those provided to other employees.

I received tons of mail celebrating the PDA victory, but I will never forget one bittersweet letter from a nurse in South Carolina. She had been promised three months' leave by her employer, who was also her obstetrician. She worked until the day she delivered but developed toxemia after giving birth. About one month after she delivered the baby, her doctor called the nurse's husband to ask him to let his wife know before she came in for her postnatal checkup that she wouldn't be getting her job back. The only protection she got under the PDA was that her disability benefits would continue until she was fully recovered. She told me how grateful she was to have her benefits but said she was heartbroken about losing the job she had had for six years. "Pregnancy and work are still like oil and water," she wrote. "Women need a guarantee that getting pregnant doesn't mean having to choose between having a baby and having a job."

When I returned to work after the birth of my children it was to a different job, one that was part-time. But the majority of today's families do not enjoy the economic flexibility I did. The average working wife contributes 28 percent of her family's annual income. Wives who work full-year, full-time jobs contribute 40 percent.[2] Increasingly, families rely on the woman's earnings. That income can make a critical difference, enabling them to own a home or to send a child to college or, in an increasing number of families, just to get by. Furthermore, women alone support about 10.2 million families—16 percent of all families in the United States.[3] This is the new reality for Americans. This is the true picture of our family life.

Several years after passing the PDA we began to address the problem of job security. After Ronald Reagan came to office, much of my time was spent fighting to keep the gains we had already made. Early in 1984, I met with the leaders of several women's organizations to discuss the possibility of introducing legislation to guarantee that women could get their jobs back after pregnancy. We hoped that a congressman who had been the author of a maternity leave law in the California legislature would introduce a *parental* leave bill. He was, however, unwilling to sponsor such a bill, preferring one that called for maternity leave only—even though the California law was being challenged in the courts because by extending benefits only to women, it discriminated against men.

For a lot of reasons I thought introducing a maternity-leave-only bill was a big mistake—a step backward. The kind of legislation I favored recognized that fathers also were parents. The California law denied fathers any rights to temporary leave to care for their newborn children and was silent about adoptive parents altogether. Nor did it acknowledge that employees other than pregnant women risked losing their jobs when they were temporarily unable to work because of a serious medical condition. Instead of parental leave I felt we needed family leave, which would extend the same job rights to all temporarily disabled employees and to all parents who must leave work temporarily to care for their children.

In 1984 and 1985, a task force headed by Georgetown law professors Wendy Williams and Sue Ross and staff attorney Donna Lenhoff from the Women's Legal Defense Fund met with my staff to draft legislation. Under the Family and Medical Leave Bill, employees could take up to eighteen weeks of unpaid, job-protected leave to care for a newborn, newly adopted, or seriously ill child. Disability leave of up to twenty-six weeks was provided to employees if they were unable to work because of a temporary serious medical condition, including pregnancy.

While we were working on this issue, Professor Edward Zigler of Yale University established an advisory panel including social policy experts Dr. Sheila Kamerman and Dr. Alfred Kahn of the Columbia School of Social Work, Dr. T. Berry Brazelton, and others, to recommend a national policy for infant-care leave. The panel endorsed a policy calling for six months of infant-care leave for all employees, three of which, they suggested, should be paid.[4]

Kahn and Kamerman had found in their research that 80 percent of women in the work force are of childbearing age, and that 93 percent of these women are likely to become pregnant during their working careers. They also found that the United States lagged far behind at least a hundred other countries in maternity-related benefits and that only 40 percent of women in the U.S. work force received benefits including partial wage replacement and job reinstatement.[5] Whenever I met with women who are parliamentarians in other parts of the world, they could not believe that the United States had no national policy to give mothers job rights.

In the fall of 1985 I was able to get congressional hearings on the issue of parental leave. It was the individual testimony from people who had lost their jobs that had the most dramatic impact on the congressional committee. We heard first from Liberia Johnson, of Charleston, South Carolina, who told the committee about being promised a six-week job-protected leave, only to discover she had been fired when she tried to make arrangements for her return to work. Next, Lorraine Poole, a prospective adoptive parent working for the city of Philadelphia, recalled her experience of waiting a year and a half to adopt a baby and then having to give it up because the maternity-leave benefit provided by the city was available only to birth mothers.

The last witness was the most unexpected. Steven Weber of the United Mine Workers introduced his testimony by saying he was sure we were all wondering what a macho union like the Mine Workers was doing there. We soon found out. Mine workers were losing their jobs because they had missed too many days of work as a result of having to travel long distances to find proper care for children of theirs who were sick with cancer.[6]

What followed the hearings was remarkable. Reporters never stopped calling. The office was flooded with inquiries, at first from female journalists who either had already had similar experiences themselves or could see what was ahead for them. The press discovered a whole new issue: parental leave. Calls and letters also came from other women across the country. Some wrote just to support my efforts to pass the bill, but what surprised me was the number of women who wrote to tell me that it had never occurred to them that they weren't covered under a maternity leave policy until they were already pregnant.

Employment policies have generally not kept pace with the changing needs of the work force, but it should be noted that some companies, like U.S. West, Eastman Kodak, and Merck, have led the way by implementing model parental leave programs. There are more employers, large and small, who offer unpaid leave than ever before. Unfortunately, the success of individual employers has not translated into widespread support—in fact, quite the opposite. The Chamber of Commerce and the National Association of Manufacturers joined forces with the National Federation for Independent Businesses and a coalition of trade associations to try to defeat my bill. Their primary reason for the fight, they said, was philosophical. They claimed that the federal government should not "mandate benefits": employers should have complete autonomy to decide matters such as when to grant leaves of absence and to whom. In numerous meetings and hearings, business representatives explained that they weren't against parental leave as a concept, but they were unanimously opposed to it as an employee's right. Some argued that employees should have the "freedom" to negotiate for this benefit or chose another. The same folks used to say coal miners should have the "freedom" to negotiate or not negotiate with their employers for mine safety.

Congress had established long ago its authority to set minimum labor standards for health and safety in the workplace. These were not benefits but minimum standards that could not be negotiated away. Organized groups of business interests have, in the past, opposed child labor legislation, minimum wage and maximum hours laws, and the Equal Pay Act. But we've learned that such legislation not only works, it is practical. If all employers have to follow the same rules, then offering an unpaid leave would not put any employer at a competitive disadvantage. In reverse, if employers can pick and choose what standards apply, then the good guys are less able to compete.

Privately, many employers have told me how much they think their parental leave policies have contributed to high morale and low turnover. They concede that a good parental leave policy helps attract the best employers. One small businessman from Denver forwarded to me a copy of a letter he had sent to his employers association, which opposed the legislation. He told the group, "Come out of the dark ages and support policies that are good for America's families and good for American business as well."

None of these issues are simple. I know how difficult it can be for a small business or office to do without even one employee. In 1987, my press secretary took a three-month parental leave to care for her newborn baby, and my committee staff director took leave to care for his two newly adopted babies. It wasn't easy for me or for the rest of the office staff, but we managed. We did what 80 percent of companies do when someone is on leave—we redistributed the work. Everyone had to push harder, but knowing how important those first few months are for new parents and their children, people pitched in and did it. I know that in some situations, where a business is working on a small margin of profit, the temporary loss of a skilled employee can have extreme repercussions. Obviously, both sides have to make accommodations. The issues can be complex, but other countries have successfully dealt with them. That is why federal legislation must lead the way.

To get enough votes to move our bill a compromise version was worked out with the chairman, William L. Clay, and with Rep. Marge Roukema, the ranking Republican on the subcommittee. The final version of the bill, now called the Family and Medical Leave Act, addressed many of the business community's concerns. The bill exempted businesses with fewer than fifty employees; after three years it would lower the number to thirty-five. An employee had to work for at least one year before becoming eligible, and family leave was reduced from eighteen weeks to ten over a two-year period. An employee could also take time off to care for a seriously ill parent. Medical leave was reduced from twenty-six to fifteen weeks in a one-year period. Employees taking either family leave or medical leave would have the right to return to the same position or a similar one, and their seniority, pension rights, and health care coverage would be maintained.

I supported the compromise but was sad about the reduction in the number of weeks for both family leave and medical leave. I knew from personal experience how devastating a difficult pregnancy can be and how long it can take to recuperate physically, not to mention emotionally. Although many pregnant women would be covered under the compromise, those women not covered would be at risk of losing their jobs at a critical time. I was also concerned that with a family leave of only ten weeks, parents trying to adopt through agencies would not be able to because many agencies require one parent be at home with the new child for a much longer period.

Obviously I didn't like raising the small employer exemption to fifty, but without that, the votes would not have been there to move the bill. It was a pity because the statistics showed that women who worked for small employers were the least likely to be unionized and the most likely to be low-paid and at a disadvantage in negotiating leave on their own. The higher exemption put more men and women than I liked beyond the reach of the legislation. Lowering the exemption to businesses with thirty-five employees after three years would help a little.

The compromise was certainly the right move politically; it brought a significant number of new supporters to the bill and created tremendous momentum for it. By the spring of 1988, forty additional Democratic members and sixteen Republicans had signed on to the bill. Of course, this didn't happen on its own. Over two hundred organizations—women's groups, health agencies, organizations for the aging, religious groups, labor unions, professional and business associations—endorsed the legislation and spent countless hours working on and off Capitol Hill to gain support. A coalition of this size and breadth demonstrated to the members just how profoundly the problem was felt. But the job was not easy. Of the hundred and fifty cosponsors signed on to the bill, only a handful were from the South or were Republican conservatives. Without such support, we wouldn't have enough votes to pass the legislation. Even though it was watered down to accommodate them, these people hoped the bill never would make it to the floor so they wouldn't have to vote on it. They kept putting obstacles in the bill's way, believing that a vote in favor would alienate business support back home. Local companies had made it clear that a "yes" vote, in their view, would be a vote *for* labor and *against* business. But it wasn't so simple. The Southerners and conservatives also knew that this was a family issue, and a vote against the bill would represent, in their districts, a vote against parents and children. No one likes to have to choose between individual constituents and business interests.

Even with its limitations, if successful, the Family and Medical Leave Act will help parents bridge the gap between work and family responsibilities by encouraging employers to establish a more responsive workplace. Over 20 million women will have job protection when they become pregnant, adopt a child, or need to stay at home with a seriously ill child. Men and women will be able to care for their dependent parents. Fathers will finally be recognized as responsible parents and their rights as such will be protected. And any employee who becomes seriously ill will not face the economic disaster of losing a job at such a difficult time. If this bill becomes law, we will be able to deal directly with some conditions that create great stress on the American family. Now all we have is seminars on "How to Cope with Stress," where we tell folks to go to a spa!

Talking about families raises some tough policy questions. If we are really going to bridge the gap between work and family and create a more responsive workplace, what is involved? How far do we go? Congressional opponents of my bill were already asking: if parental leave now, what next? *Paid* parental leave, mandated sick leave, pension benefits, health insurance coverage, child care? The same kind of argument is made against any progressive legislation. People said, when child labor laws were passed, that the next step would be the federal government's forbidding parents to give kids chores.

We can't walk away from the hard issues. Much remains to be done if the needs of families are going to be addressed. The fight for parental leave legislation has attracted a dynamic coalition on its behalf. We have to counter the old scare arguments that have always been used with the good common sense that has always been our strong point.

5
Child Care

WHEN I arrived in Congress, I had the usual freshman jitters about how I would ever juggle committee meetings, votes, district visits, receptions, floor debates. . . . As it turned out, I found learning the ropes in Congress a snap compared with arranging child care for two young children! That first year in Washington I had half a dozen different arrangements, including housekeepers, baby-sitters, and a child care center. I needed a contingency plan for seven days a week, twenty-four hours a day.

I would take the children with me when I was on a plane, and I was amazed to find that my colleagues simply "didn't see" us. We say we are a child-oriented society, but show up with a child, and adults come out with the darnedest things. If I took one of the children to a meeting, someone would invariably ask, "What's that?"

When I was interviewed during my first term, I was always asked what was my biggest fear as a freshman in Congress. I'd answer, "Losing my housekeeper." I figured I could cope with almost anything, but that my life would go into free fall if she left. It was an answer that reporters did not often get. I was very fortunate to have the money for a housekeeper. It spared me the worry and the guilt that many of my working friends had.

And luckily, my own mother was very spunky in defending working women. She was a great role model. Once, when she was campaigning for me in Denver, a women she had never seen before came down off her front porch and shouted: "I won't support Pat Schroeder because she's a bad mother. Mothers should stay home with their kids!"

My mother swallowed and said, "Well, I was a working mother and my children turned out great."

"Oh yeah?" the woman said incredulously. "What do your poor kids do now?"

"Well, the boy is a prominent attorney in Denver, and the girl is Pat Schroeder!"

My children are grown now, but when I see young parents who are doing the best they can to juggle work and family obligations, my bones empathize. It's a demanding act that calls for the timing of a ringmaster, the humor of a clown, the tenacity of a lion tamer, and the grace of a trapeze artist. The energy required is phenomenal.

The reality of being a working parent sinks in after parental leave is over, when it is time to return to work. All at once, parents have to find child care and go through the trauma of leaving their babies and readjusting to their jobs. Knowing how difficult this is, in my first press conference after my election in 1973 I joined other members of Congress urging passage of a bill that would do something about the lack of affordable child care in America. Reporters kept firing questions at me because I was their story: "the young working mother in Congress with two preschool children." Fifteen years have passed, my children are now college-age, the 1973 bill didn't pass, and the same battle continues. Little progress has been made and the basic need has grown more pressing each year.

Child care options continue to be scarce. Over five million children under age five need child care, but no serious effort to keep up with the demand has been made by the states, the federal government, or business. In California, at this writing, there are only eight thousand child care slots for the five hundred thousand eligible children. A similar shortfall is common in every community in the United States.[1]

Trying to find good care creates terrific stress for working families. Some of them give up because of the emotional and financial costs and try to get by on one income until their kids are older. But many parents don't have that option. They are forced to spend huge amounts of time, money, and energy trying to find a solution. Family finances often dictate they must make do with a situation they are not comfortable with. Children may end up at inadequate or even dangerous child care facilities. Mothers and fathers leave for work in the morning feeling worried and insecure about their children, but with no other options available to them.

Why is this common situation, created by lack of adequate child care, ignored and allowed to grow worse each year? One reason is that our society cannot decide how to treat the working woman. We have considered child care a "women's" issue rather than what it really is: a family issue. Our ambivalence stems from two deep-rooted biases: first, we believe that people should not have children unless they can "afford" them; and second, we feel mothers should stay at home with their young children. We are angry that welfare mothers have babies they can't support, and we urge them to go out and get jobs immediately. They can almost never find or afford first-rate child care, but we say they must work anyway, and then we blame the mothers if the children don't do well in school or get into trouble because of "poor parental supervision." Basically, we are saying to such a mother that she should not have had the child.

We also give middle-class mothers a double message. We imply that their kids will suffer irreparable harm if the mothers *don't* stay home. Yet if the family cannot afford a home, a car, college, and health insurance, we make the parents feel they have short-changed their children. If the mother goes to work because these expenses overload the family budget, we say: Don't ask us to help with quality child care; pay your own way *and* take care of the kids yourself. The government doesn't belong in family economics. In fact, the government ends up penalizing middle-class families. That is because many legislators believe that women will abandon their homes for jobs if we make finding child care too easy. Everyone knows women are dying for two full-time jobs!

I think this is the real roadblock to getting action on the child care crisis. Politicians are afraid that if they address the problem they will be blamed when women get jobs outside the home. In 1892, when Chicago was preparing for an exposition celebrating the four-hundredth anniversary of Christopher Columbus's discovery of America, a group of women built a child care facility adjacent to the premises. A Chicago newspaper was enraged. It ranted in its editorials that women from all over America would come, leave their children in day care, and never return for them. Chicago would be swamped with orphans. Well, not one child was left, but unfortunately that attitude still prevails almost one hundred years later.

Many conservatives believe that the only people who should have children are those who can afford to have one parent stay home and do the chores. If that were the case, a small percentage of American families would have children. We would die out! If medical science could make octogenarians fertile, then I suppose by the time we were eighty we could all finance families in the "traditional" way. Unfortunately, medical science isn't there yet.

To make progress on child care we must bury these cultural biases. Middle-class women are in the workplace because they want the same things for their families that they themselves had as children. Imagine! What the Schroeder family paid for our first house is not enough to buy a new car in today's market. Salaries have not kept pace with rising costs. As I have said before, feminism did not push women out of the home, family finances did.

Many people believe that those who "choose" to work don't deserve any assistance in their effort to balance work and family. They see the choice of working outside the home solely as a life-style decision and not as an economic issue. As one woman wrote, "I prefer not to make it easier for working women to turn child-raising duties over to surrogate mothers."

I find this attitude offensive. Woman should not be punished if they want to work. The fact that it is their choice does not diminish their need for child care or some other support system. In addition, we should not forget that government statistics tell us that only one woman in ten will get through life with the option to decide whether she "wants" to work. The other nine will *have* to work. To say, "Let's make all welfare mothers work" and, at the same time, to treat all other working mothers as upper-middle-class people in pursuit of a Mercedes doesn't make sense. We must continually emphasize that.

It has always interested me that no one questions whether a man is working as a matter of choice or of economic necessity. We take it for granted that, in most cases, it's a little of both. Mothers should be weighed in the same scale as fathers. But fathers do not have an easy go either, for society is uncertain how to deal with men who want more time with their families. It has been said that we'll know men have been liberated when a man dies saying that he wishes he'd spent more time at the office!

When my husband, Jim, was in high school, his father, a dentist in suburban Chicago, wasn't able to attend any of his football games because he was always working. Today, fathers try to schedule business meetings so that they don't interfere with their sons' school play or their daughters' soccer game. More fathers are demanding time to be with their families, and many employers are having trouble responding to those requests.

Today, both parents confront the stressful challenge of balancing the demands of work with the needs of their children. One out of every four workers—man or woman—worries about child care while at work. Statistics show that both parents lose some time from work because of child care emergencies. A 1986 AT&T study revealed that 77 percent of women and 73 percent of men with children under age eighteen dealt with family issues on company time.[2]

Both parents go through the anxiety of finding the right place to leave their kids. No matter how relieved you are about finally lining up child care, the first time you drop your child off is always heart-wrenching. When I was in New Hampshire in 1988 on the Great American Family tour, a young mother came up to the microphone at one of our meetings and asked Dr. Brazelton if it was normal to be as upset and confused as she felt when she returned to work. The pain of the separation was apparent as she tearfully told us how it broke her heart to take her baby to the child care center. "It's . . . just . . . so . . . hard," she sobbed.

I detect the same sense of trauma in the letters young mothers write, as they tell of feeling torn by working and placing their child in someone else's care. "My mom didn't work and was always there for me" they say, or "I miss watching my child grow up."

Such statements are symptoms of what Dr. Brazelton describes in his book *Working and Caring* as the grieving process mothers and fathers go through when they face child care.[3] As he told that woman in New Hampshire, the process is normal. But, he said, "I worry about how the separation affects the development of the parents more than how it affects the babies."

If we finally started to help young families handle their work and child care obligations instead of blaming them for needing help, a lot of stress and guilt would be alleviated. Young families have no breathing room to enjoy their parenthood. They are immediately in a child care crisis. I think the stress contributes to our very high divorce rate. Having a child is, under these circumstances, not much fun.

For women who are able to leave their jobs to stay home and care for their children, life is not easy either. They don't experience the daily separation from the child, but they do have to readjust to their new circumstances. There is a lingering misconception that homemakers have all the time in the world to do whatever they please. They don't. Their job is not easy, and their hard work unfortunately remains undervalued. Many of these mothers also worry about whether they made the right choice in staying home, feel guilty that they aren't adding extra income to the family bank account, and try to stretch the single paycheck their husband brings home. Some also worry about the divorce rate. Many women are one husband away from poverty. Women's magazines remind them of this frequently. Others are depressed because they miss interacting with adults and are no longer able to pursue their life work. While many are happy with their choice, some are not. One woman wrote me, "I feel so uninteresting."

Today's young mothers have a much tougher time than I did when I had my family twenty-five years ago. Although I valued my career, I had no second thoughts about quitting work to stay home with my young children. In that economy, we could live on one salary without fearing that the house would be repossessed. I could find part-time work, something that is so hard to come by today. There was less competition for good child care than there is now, and part-time child care was much easier to find.

But even then there was no simple solution to the child care problem. My options, like those of so many working parents today, included placing the children in someone else's home (family care), having a baby-sitter come to our home, or taking the children to a center. My child care experience was a mixture of all of the above.

Interviewing a prospective baby-sitter or choosing a child care center is a difficult emotional experience. Parents often cite their "gut reaction" as a key factor in their decision. They may have done a great deal of careful research, but often it comes down to a question of trust as they ask themselves, "Will my child be safe here?" And they soon find out that children learn to scream their loudest just as you are going out the door. They know how to instill guilt. I used to phone a few minutes after I left and was always surprised to hear that the screaming had stopped as rapidly as it began. If Academy Awards were given for Best Child Actor in a Parental Good-bye Scene, the competition would be intense!

I started to work part-time after Jamie was born. My parents had moved to Denver and they took care of the kids sometimes, as did an older couple who had befriended us. However, both these households were clear across town. To manage, we needed to find something nearby. Determined to be methodical, I went down to the state agency handling child care and got the list of licensed day-care centers and family operators. Beginning with the *A*'s, I proceeded to call each of the listings. Some were no longer operating, and most were no longer taking new children. In frustration, I stopped calling somewhere around the *P*'s and decided to be creative. I typed up notices, with pictures of my kids, that said, "We need friends," and posted them at churches and apartment buildings in our neighborhood. I offered college and law school students room and board in return for evening and weekend baby-sitting. I then juggled my team of baby-sitters so that I was covered each time I had to teach or argue a case. If one of the kids got a cold, or a baby-sitter got sick or had an exam, the whole system threatened to collapse. To me, each week involved the careful execution of complex logistics. To the kids, it was a week chock-full of outings with different friends.

My patchwork arrangement continued until I ran for Congress. Then, because I was out campaigning many nights, Jim stepped in and handled things on the home front. I told him, "You don't want to travel around and have to look attentive while you listen to me give the same speech over and over." He agreed and I campaigned alone. In my absence, he became a better father. When we both were around, I tended to be the "keeper" of the children, but now the children saw that he was just as able as Mom—and probably more fun. When Jim discusses this experience with his friends, he says he realizes how few of them actually talk to their children. Men tell him that they envy his relationships with Jamie and Scott. Our situation forced him to become actively involved. Rather than causing problems, it brought our family closer together and allowed the children to know their father much better.

Life has been a juggling act for both of us, as it is for so many other parents. We've tried to strike our own balance between work and family. I did, though, go through a time when I thought I had to do everything and do it well. I tried to be the type-E mother—everything to everyone. Very soon I found that super-mom equals guilty mom!

Many times I felt I had to be in two places at once. Sometimes I brought the kids to the office (Jamie was virtually toilet-trained in the House rest rooms) and other times I elicited emergency help from neighbors and friends. When the local florist asked me why I sent so many flower arrangements to other women in the neighborhood, I explained, "I'm just a guilty working mother!"

Working mothers must be creative and resourceful. I rarely got to the grocery before midnight. We had Jamie's fourth birthday party transported to Capitol Hill because the House was still in session and I couldn't get away. I had to call the House security office with special instructions: "Yes, a clown will be coming in. Red hair. That's right." On another occasion I didn't have time to buy birthday party favors so I froze ice cubes of colored water with quarters inside, wrapped them up, and passed them out to our party guests. I recommend this only if the children are old enough *not* to swallow the quarters.

We all had to learn to be more honest with one another. I said to the kids: "Tell me when you need me. Tell me what you want me to do. I don't read minds."

One incident made me realize that striving to be a perfect mommy was ridiculous. One day Scott told me that he needed a cake for a school bake sale. Baking is not one of my strong suits, but despite the fact that I had a stack of papers to go through, I baked a cake. The next night I had to ask Scott how the cake had gone over at school. "Oh, it was fine," he said distractedly, "but most of the kids brought money." I realized then that Scott hadn't cared one way or another whether I made a cake, bought a cake, or sent money. It was my problem, not his. At that point, I tossed out my *Joy of Cooking* and replaced it with a list of restaurants and bakeries that deliver.

Parents can get needlessly overwrought about little things and be too harsh on themselves. When I gave up my aspirations to become supermom, a lot of stress blew away. As my children got older and I became busier, I tried to incorporate them into my work world as much as possible. I also tried to make their time *away* from me as interesting and as much fun as possible. One fall I arranged for them to spend a weekend in New England with friends so that they could see the autumn leaves. A colleague of mine happened to be on the plane with Scott and Jamie and was startled that these two young children were by themselves. "Where are your parents?" he asked. The kids answered in a matter-of-fact tone, "Oh, Mom is in Geneva, Dad is in Thailand, and we're on our way to Boston to see the leaves change." They seemed to take pride in their independence.

They got used to my job and viewed my staff as a sort of extended family. The blending of the two worlds made such an impression on Jamie that when she was eight, she surveyed her fellow third-graders on the topic of work and family. She found that, like her, most of her classmates didn't live in the same town as their grandparents, aunts, and uncles. At their dinner tables they heard about their parents' co-workers, and they felt they knew them. Jamie testified before the White House Conference on Families about her survey, pointing out that the kids wanted to see what their parents did during the day. Parents visit school, but most kids don't visit work!

While it won't solve the problem of child care, linking the two worlds of work and family life can make workers more productive and the workplace a more efficient, less stressful environment. Unfortunately, a large segment of the corporate world believes that children should be invisible, except once a year at the company picnic. The traditional corporate ethos holds that all family matters should be kept private.

That's absurd. Workers, mothers *and* fathers, shouldn't be expected to treat their children as secrets or to take care of their families' needs behind closed doors. Obviously, you can't have children running around an office or a plant floor. You *can*, however, do what many European and Japanese, and increasingly more American, companies do: provide on-site child care, offer family counseling services, tailor vacation schedules to family needs, and make other such accommodations. If employees are preoccupied with their home problems at work, it's the employer who is hurt.

One reason changes in the workplace have been slow in coming is that our society is still, to an overwhelming degree, governed by older upper-middle-class white men who know little of the family balancing act because their wives have insulated them from it. To such men family issues are too soft and sentimental and don't belong in the no-nonsense world of work. Home and family are harbors of tranquillity they retreat to. Dual-income families don't find the same tranquillity at home!

As part of my work on the House Armed Services Committee, I talk to generals who tell me privately that their number-one personnel problem is inadequate child care for the families of service people in their command. Enlisted men and women cite family issues as among their primary concerns and many say that these problems are the key determinant as to whether or not they will reenlist. Family issues also affect the readiness of our armed forces. I remember one base commander telling me that he had to alert his soldiers of a "surprise" exercise so that they could make sure that they had child care lined up. Still, these men say nothing publicly about such concerns in committee hearings. They, too, fear being labeled soft if they push family issues. We must make it okay for men to deal with family issues if we are to speed up progress.

Those who manage the workplace, whether in the military or in a Fortune 500 company, have to change their attitudes and develop policies that are more responsive to families. Sometimes all it takes is just one person in a position of power to start the ball rolling. My friend Gary David Goldberg, executive producer of *Family Ties*, did just that when he used the leverage of renegotiating his contract with Paramount Studios as a means to get an on-site child care center. Paramount is now among the most efficient studios in the history of Hollywood and the child care center is one of the reasons why.

I don't think there are enough powerful executives who see child care as a bottom-line issue for their companies. The questions are not easy to deal with, and companies have a right to be cautious about jumping into areas they know nothing about. But adjusting the balance between work and family is a national task that must get done. It will require employees who aren't afraid to speak out about their child care problems, and enlightened executives who understand and value the benefits of helping employees cope with conflicting responsibilities. It's important to note here that employers are sometimes unaware of the problems their workers are having with child care. That is because employees hesitate to mention the situation for fear they will define themselves as "marginal," as people who are too distracted to do a good job. We have to bring this situation out of the closet so both employers and employees can take some positive action.

Some businesses are becoming more responsive. Large corporations like IBM and Honeywell and smaller companies like B&B Associates, a Connecticut graphic design and printing firm, are examining how they can help the people who work for them meet their child care responsibilities. According to national groups that monitor employer-supported child care, only a small percentage of private companies offer child care assistance, but the number of employers who provide some form of help has increased significantly during the last ten years. For example, in 1978, The Conference Board, an employer-supported research group based in New York, estimates that approximately 3,500 companies are providing their employees with some type of child care support. And from talking to various business groups around the country, I know that interest in employer-supported child care programs continues to rise. But there are obstacles—costs, liability, and the shortage of technical assistance are the three mentioned most often by managers. The hurdles are particularly high for smaller companies. As an Atlanta businesswoman told me, "Child care was essential to me when I was starting out in the work force. Now that I own a company, I would love to provide child care as a benefit to my employees. But I just can't make the numbers work."

For American companies, the most popular approach to helping parents care for their children has been the establishment of flexible personnel policies: such programs as flexitime, part-time work schedules, flexplace, job sharing, and flexible leave. The programs vary: flexitime allows an employee to choose, within constraints set by the employer, the time when he or she arrives at and departs from work. In job sharing, two people share the responsibilities of one full-time job and prorate the salary and benefits. Increasingly, enlightened employers are offering plans like these.

Obviously some kinds of jobs can accommodate these policies more easily than others, where complex arrangements are required. As an employer who instituted flexitime in my own office, I can attest to the fact that adjustments are necessary. My press secretary, who has a young toddler and an hour's commute, comes in to work an hour later than my other staff and stays an extra hour at night. It works out fine except on those busy mornings when reporters are calling for reactions to the latest political story and my aide is not there to help field the calls. Exasperating times like these, however, are outweighed by the benefit of keeping a seasoned press person on staff.

According to a San Francisco research organization, Hewlett-Packard, Levi Strauss, AT&T, Wells Fargo Bank, the Illinois,

Mountain, and Pacific Bell companies, and the states of New York and California have all used flexible work schedules and have been satisfied with the results. They have found that there is reduced turnover, better morale, greater job satisfaction and productivity, lower absentee rates, and retention of valued employees.[4] For example, at Hewlett-Packard, managers reported that because of their flexitime program, absenteeism has decreased and tardiness has been almost eliminated. Another company, Security Life of Denver, found that its flexitime program boosted employee morale, kept the office open longer hours, and at the same time allowed individual employees more time off.

But the real point is that children are our most valuable national resource. Taking good care of them is a national responsibility—for parents, for employers, for all of us.

The federal government has provided a model for private companies by creating more flexible work options for federal employees. As chairwoman of the House Civil Service Subcommittee, I found it exciting to witness this change. In 1975, when I took over the Census and Population Subcommittee, I conducted hearings on ways to increase the productivity of the federal work force. We heard testimony that one path toward getting more efficient workers was to give them more control over their schedules. What we were told over and over again was that people can't do their best when they are worrying about who is with their children. As a result of those hearings, I introduced a pilot flexitime program for federal workers. I was surprised at how much resistance there was at first, but we were, after all, challenging the normal patterns of work. Because it was a demonstration program, employees, managers, and members of Congress were willing to give it a chance, and the program was passed into law. The pilot was such a success that Congress made flexitime permanent, with six out of eleven agencies reporting greater efficiency and overwhelming support from employees and managers. As one manager told me, "It should no longer be an experiment. It should be a way of life."

The legislation served as a catalyst for more experimentation with alternative work schedules in the federal government. But most important, it set an example for the private sector, helping to demonstrate that the workplace could accommodate family schedules and become more productive at the same time.

I was especially proud of pushing through, in 1978, the Federal Employees Part-time Career Employment Act, a law that created ten thousand new part-time jobs in the federal government. From personal experience, I knew what a boon this would be to working mothers who wanted to ease back gradually into the work force. Part-time employment had helped me to keep my skills current as I cut back on my work to spend more time with my kids. I understand, however, that for many people, part-time work is not an attractive career alternative because it means lower wages, fewer fringe benefits, and limited advancement opportunities. Many employers regard part-timers as second-class workers rather than bona fide members of the work force who may have special skills and experience to contribute. One reason I made certain that my legislation included prorated benefits was to counter this stereotype and recognize that part-time employees, in spite of their shorter hours, are an essential segment of the federal work force.

As important as flexible work options are, however, child care remains the centerpiece of a responsive workplace. From what I have seen, it is also the issue parents identify most often as crucial to their lives. While there has been a sharp increase in the number of businesses that have done something about child care, most companies still are much more likely to give employees a parking space for a car than to provide a child care slot for a son or daughter. The Employee Benefits Research Institute, a Washington public policy organization, predicts that child care will be "the employee benefit of the 1990s." In order for this to happen, employers have to understand better the range of available options. For many corporate executives, the term "child care" conjures up an expensive on-site center with high insurance rates and complicated building codes. Most managers don't realize they can offer some child care benefits that are relatively inexpensive and are not burdensome. These include courses to teach parents how to find and evaluate providers; child care resource and referral services to help parents find good child care; and salary redirection programs, under which specific amounts of money from employee paychecks are withheld, deposited into accounts to pay child care expenses, and subtracted from the employee's taxable income.

During my travels, I have been impressed by the creativity and commitment to their employees some businesses have shown in tackling child care problems. In Phoenix, Arizona, the president of Air West proudly told me of his airline's child care initiatives. They had hired family care providers, trained them, and made them employees of the airline, complete with flight benefits. Flight attendants from other airlines talk about the program enviously. Children receive good care, the parents have peace of mind, and the child care mothers earn health insurance and other fringe benefits. Success stories like this one are important because they show that businesses can ease the pressure on working parents and operate more efficiently themselves.

The Congressional Caucus for Women's Issues, which I co-chair, recently launched the Child Care Challenge, a campaign to focus attention on creative child care programs. We asked members of Congress to submit examples of how employers and communities in their districts meet the child care challenge. We then compiled and printed these case studies and distributed them to the public. We also distributed the case studies to business schools, in the hope that they might include them in their management courses.

Fox Television produced a video of the winning examples of these creative child care solutions. They included a consortium of businesses in Dallas, Texas, that provides child care in its business park; a nursing home in Kansas that houses a day-care center and offers an opportunity for the young and the old to interact; and a bank in California that has a holiday and summer program for its employees' school-age children. We gave the videos to members of Congress who participated, asking them to pass them along to employers in their districts so that they could see the wide range of solutions bubbling up all over America.

All these approaches pay off, resulting in a decrease in tardiness, stress, employee turnover, and absenteeism, as well as an increase in morale and productivity. I don't think, though, that employers can or should be expected to shoulder the responsibility of child care alone. I'm not advocating a return to the paternalistic days of the 1920s when company towns and company houses sprang up all across America and your company *was* your family. But it is time that businesses do more than they have been doing and become active partners with employees and government in dealing with child care. Communities, as well as state and federal government, must also join in and invest both money and commitment.

Child care, whether it's for infants, toddlers, schoolchildren, or handicapped or sick children, poses a major crisis for many families. While the great infusion of women into the permanent labor force in recent years has created a demographic revolution, we are not the first generation that has had to deal with mothers who work outside the home. In World War II, when women had to take men's places in the factories as part of the war effort, the government sponsored and operated child care centers. Whether government centers are the solution or not, American families today deserve that same level of commitment. Yet no comprehensive policy exists. Just as in the question of parental leave, the United States lags behind other industrialized countries in attempts to make life easier for working parents.

In the long run, child care is the parents' responsibility. But there is no future for a country that ignores the needs of its children. Government should lead the way to create a framework for many child care options. We must do something to increase the number of family day care homes and centers in order to broaden the range of choices and options for parents. I also think we have a special obligation to help defray the costs for low-income families so that they can afford quality child care and have the chance to earn a living. The alternative, a situation that we see every day, is that low-income families who cannot provide child care fall out of the work force and onto the welfare rolls. For low-income parents, affordable child care can mean the difference between working and welfare. A 1983 Census Bureau study found that over a third of mothers in families with incomes less than $15,000 a year said they would look for work if they could find child care at a reasonable cost. In states such as Florida and Massachusetts vigorous efforts to provide poor mothers with child care services have cut welfare rolls by half.[5]

To get a handle on the crisis, we must deal with several basic problems that plague our current ad hoc system. First, there is the problem of regulating child care facilities. Most of our providers are not licensed. Informal arrangements with friends and relatives—the most frequently used type of child care—are extremely difficult to regulate. We've all been terrorized by baby-sitters we thought we could trust. I'll never forget the one I trusted to take care of the children one weekend who then hired another baby-sitter—one we did not know—to watch them while we were gone. I was furious that she was so cavalier.

It's especially awkward for parents to keep questioning friends and neighbors about the children, but parents should not be intimidated. Often they don't even ask questions, feeling that if they hear bad news, they have no other option anyway. Parents have a right and a responsibility to know about the people providing care, and the setting that is a part of their children's day, and they should have several safe choices. A recent disastrous fire in a New York apartment where several "day" children were killed is an extreme example of the tragedy of unsafe care. Certainly, any household that is used for baby-sitting or care of more than three children should be carefully regulated.

Obviously, safety is the most compelling argument for licensing homes and other child care facilities. The consequences of no regulation can be tragic, as in the case of Jessica McClure, who fell into an open well at her family day-care home, and in the recent child abuse cases in centers across the country. For many parents it is just luck that their children have not been part of these statistics. We cannot rely on luck.

State and local governments have the primary responsibility for regulating child care facilities, but procedures and standards vary from state to state. A few states do not have any regulation. Some have argued that stricter standards will drive good providers out of the market and discourage employer-supported child care. Experience indicates otherwise in those states with strong standards—where facilities are inspected for safety, the backgrounds and qualifications of providers are investigated, the number of children per adult is specified, and the daily program is stipulated. Minnesota, for example, with some of the strongest standards in the country, has more licensed providers than states with weaker standards. As for employers, their centers adhere to rigorous standards largely because of the requirements of their liability insurance.

The federal government must declare that ensuring the safety, health, and welfare of children in any child care setting is a national priority. Minimum standards, at the very least, must be set. We want the planes we fly to be safe, drugs and food to be pure, and day care to be secure.

Second, there is the question of wages and benefits. Child care providers and teachers are grossly underpaid. Only one half of all child care workers receive health benefits, and their average annual earnings can be as low as $4,800 for those working in family day-care centers and between $10,000 and $12,000 for those in educational institutions. We pay parking-lot attendants more. Despite an average of fourteen years of education, these people are in the lowest 5 percent of all wage earners in the United States.[6] We are asking them to make a personal sacrifice to subsidize the system. Low pay fuels the industry's unusually high turnover rate—double the rate in other occupations. Frequent changes of care-givers put stress on the child, who continually has to get used to someone new; it's also hard on parents, who must start their search again from scratch. Low wages also make it difficult to attract the kind of people most of us want to watch over our children. To get qualified and trained workers will mean raising the cost of child care for everyone, and that may very well require additional government subsidies to keep the system going. A third major issue is the affordability of child care. Pre-school programs, so important to a child's early development, are prohibitively expensive for many families. As a result, many poor children start school with an educational handicap. Nursery school enrollment for four-year-olds was 67 percent in 1985 for children whose parents earned over $35,000. It was only 33 per-cent for children whose parents earned under $10,000.[7]

There have been efforts by federal and state governments, as well as by some businesses, to offer educational opportunities to more young children. In 1965, the federal government funded the Head Start program to give disadvantaged children access to enriched early childhood education. Head Start is a good example of an effective and cost-efficient preschool program. The Select Committee on Children, Youth, and Families in 1988 found that every dollar invested in the program returns six dollars in savings. Children who have been in Head Start are more likely to finish school and become employable rather than depending on public assistance. There is also an apparent correlation between crime statistics and enrollment in the program: according to studies presented before the Select Committee, children in Head Start are less likely to be arrested later for delinquent and criminal activity than are other youngsters from similar life situations.[8]

When it was time to enroll Jamie in preschool, we both visited many programs, and Jamie was sold on Head Start. Because she wasn't an economically disadvantaged child, the county had to give me a special waiver so that I could pay to enroll her. The program's goal was to make the children self-sufficient, a welcome contrast to Scott's middle-class preschool program, which tended to coddle the children. Jamie's class learned how to do things that many adults, myself included, didn't know how to do—like cleaning fish. Jamie loved the program. The children in her class were poor, but she never knew it. As far as she was concerned, they all had one thing in common—their mothers worked.

Parental involvement is key to the success of Head Start. Parents are partners in the children's educational experience. I tried to make sure my congressional schedule allowed me to participate as much as the other mothers did. Once, the class was going to the National Portrait Gallery and the teacher thought it would be exciting for the students if their own pictures could be taped to the walls next to some of the exhibits. My job was to convince the director. We did it, and the children were thrilled.

Despite the program's success and its proven capacity to prevent difficulties later in a child's life, funding for Head Start has not kept up with the demand. It serves only 16 percent of eligible children. Over the past several years, the federal government has added only slightly more money for the program. When inflation and the increase in the number of poor children are factored in, the amount of funding per child has actually gone down. Money has not been available to hire new staff, expand the program, or raise salaries to attract and keep qualified teachers. A stellar program like Head Start deserves much more support. It is shameful and senseless that we do not nourish a proven program that reinforces families and children.

Some state governments have supplemented Head Start with preschool programs for four-year-olds. South Carolina began such a program in 1984 and now serves about 60 percent of all "at-risk" four-year-olds. Senator Edward Kennedy has come up with a proposal, "Smart Start," that offers federal matching grants to states that establish similar programs on a full-day, year-round basis. Half the spaces would be reserved for poor kids, at no cost to their parents, while those with higher incomes would pay on a sliding scale. To me this is an important feature because I strongly believe that we should not set poor children apart from middle- and upper-class kids. As I know from Jamie's Head Start experience, everyone learns from the interaction.

There are also innovative preschool programs sponsored by employers. Some businesses are working with local school districts in setting up on-site satellite schools. The American Bankers Insurance Group in Miami has in its facilities a kindergarten that is operated by the Dade County school district. Twelve companies in Dade County offer on-site public schools up to the second grade. The county saves money (approximately $219,000 for every classroom it does not have to build), and the companies retain productive workers, who can take the kids to work with them, deposit them in school, and pick them up when they leave at the end of the day.[9]

Beyond the problems of preschool care, policymakers must also address the need for other types of child care, particularly for infants, school-age (or latchkey) children, and sick and handicapped children.

Infant day care is the most in demand and the most expensive because babies simply need more attention than older children. For example, the suggested ratio for infant care is one adult to every four babies; for preschoolers, it's one to twelve. Recently, while I was in line at the grocery store, I overheard a woman telling a friend that the first week she placed ads in the paper for her new day-care service, she was flooded with calls from mothers with babies as young as three weeks old. The woman, who had planned to take in only one infant and some preschoolers, recounted that these mothers were pleading with her to take "just one more baby."

In 1986, a study by Dr. Jay Belsky, a developmental psychologist from the University of Pennsylvania, stirred up new controversy about infant care when it seemed to show that infant child care could have some negative effects on the babies. Yet parents have little choice. Despite the controversy, over 52 percent of working women have a child under the age of one in child care.

As I mentioned in the previous chapter, a national parental leave policy could help curb the demand for infant day care, as well as give parents time to bond with their babies. It would also give parents the time they need to find a comfortable child care situation. However, our policies must supplement parental leave by sparking the creation of more child care for babies, whether it's through tax incentives for businesses that make special efforts to provide infant care or through subsidies or no-interest loans for providers who agree to become licensed and trained.

By definition, you only need infant care for eleven months, but the problem of child care for older children after school hours can last for years. For example, kids may be too young to be totally responsible for themselves, yet too old to check in with a baby-sitter. Between one fourth and one third of all students who entered school in 1986 are alone from the end of the school day until their parents come home. This "latchkey" problem also has an impact on business. Dana Friedman of The Conference Board refers to "the three o'clock syndrome," the reduced productivity that occurs about the time many working parents call to make sure their children have made it home safely.[10] Latchkey parents also have the highest rates of absenteeism, according to Harry Freeman, executive vice-president of American Express, who testified before the Select Committee on Children, Youth, and Families.[11]

I coped with my latchkey problem by putting in place a network of neighbors, friends, and baby-sitters. I also tried to teach my kids survival skills—how to call the police, and, just as important for me, how to call the taxicab service. If the kids needed to go to a school function, or if some emergency came up, they were to call me and then a cab. We were lucky to live in a supportive community and to be able to afford this kind of solution to transportation problems. Obviously, not everyone can manage this way. A mother in New York described how she would take her lunch hour at three in the afternoon so she could dash on the subway to her daughter's school, pick her up, and deliver her to her play group. Workers recently transferred to new cities have told me of their fears about how their children will fare in the neighborhood. They don't know their neighbors, the children don't yet have friends, and, as a result, the family as well as the job suffers.

Schools have become more involved and have initiated before- and after-school programs that allow children to stay at school and participate in activities until their parents can pick them up. In 1984, Wellesley College developed legislation that I introduced in Congress to give grants to communities to start up such programs. I thought this was a commonsense and cost-effective bill because it let the community decide the type of program it wanted, as well as where to have it. The bill passed and became part of the Dependent Care Block Grant program that funds not only before- and after-school programs, but also community-based information and referral services on available child care.

Sick children pose a different kind of challenge for parents and employers. A feverish child can cause even the most carefully planned child care arrangements to go awry. I have heard some mothers and fathers swear that kids get sick only when there are deadlines to meet or conferences to attend. I could add: bills to debate and speeches to give. I remember sitting, between votes, with another congressman in the House dining room, mixing Scott's medicine with ice cream to disguise its bad taste. I was able to keep a blanket and pillow in my office closet in case one of my kids got sick, but most parents can't. To be more accurate, I should probably say "most *mothers* can't," since it is still mostly Mom who stays home under these circumstances. A normal child has between six and ten illnesses a year, lasting on average five to seven days. That can amount to a lot of time away from work, and many parents would put their jobs in jeopardy if they stayed out that much.

What to do? Parents are in a double bind because some day-care centers don't allow children to come when they are sick.

Grandparents often work or live in other cities. Neighbors and friends are also away during the day. Rather than see their absenteeism shoot sky-high, some businesses have supported a variety of programs: family day-care homes are recruited by the company to care for the sick children of its employees; nurse's aides are sometimes hired to go to the employees' homes to care for sick children. A Washington, D.C., law firm hired a secretary who was also a trained nurse, and if an employee's child got sick, she was prepared to step in. Obviously, this kind of solution is in limited use and is not available to most working parents.

Imagine how these problems are compounded for the parents of handicapped children. There are few facilities that will accept kids with special needs, and fewer still that are qualified to do so. Other countries—Holland, for example—have instituted creative programs for working with such children that help individual families and the society as a whole.

We need to study the ways other countries handle the problems of child care. We need to apply Yankee ingenuity to competing with other nations not only in making semiconductors but also in improving working conditions.

Despite the problems, I am amazed and encouraged at parents' resilience in managing their child care circumstances. Even without substantial government help, they are doing a remarkable job. Imagine what would happen if federal, state, and local governments joined forces with business to come up with a policy for first-rate, affordable, and accessible child care!

I think it can be done. While at present the United States government has no comprehensive child care policy, it has taken some steps to help through the Title XX Social Services Block Grant, a couple of tax breaks, and a few small, scattered child care programs. The Title XX Social Services Block Grant (referred to simply as Title XX) is a $2.7 billion entitlement the federal government gives to the states for human services. It is the largest source of direct federal aid for child care. States rely heavily on this money to fund their subsidized child care services. When

Title XX suffered deep cuts during the Reagan years, states were forced to cut back on child care. More than half the states spend less money and serve fewer children today than they did in 1981.

Most of the federal government's effort on child care has been indirect and through tax subsidies. The Dependent Care Tax Credit allows working parents to deduct from their federal income taxes up to $2,400 for the cost of child care for one child or $4,800 for two or more children. In 1986, 8.5 million families used the credit and deducted over $3.6 billion.[12]

There is also a flexible benefit or "cafeteria" plan tax subsidy, known as salary redirection. Under this provision, people who work with a participating employer may have their employer withhold up to $5,000 of their salary and place it in a special account to pay child care expenses. They can then reduce their taxable income by the same amount. Tax credits obviously aren't much help to poor families with low tax bills. Families with low incomes need direct assistance to help with their child care costs.

During 1988, Congress, for the first time in sixteen years, considered proposals for a comprehensive child care system that would provide direct assistance. The debate was crystallized by the introduction of two pieces of legislation that share the same underlying premise: the federal government should be out front in pushing for more child care options for American families. The two bills mirrored the ongoing differences between liberals and conservatives about the extent of federal participation in child care and, from that, the setting of national standards, the amount of financial support, and the use of tax benefits.

The Act for Better Child Care, or ABC bill, set the tone for the debate. Supported and developed by a range of child advocacy organizations, the bill would funnel federal dollars directly to the states to help low- and moderate-income families pay for child care services. In order to be eligible for funds, the states would have to match 20 percent of the federal money and within five years adopt minimum child care standards. States could use the money to expand Head Start programs, pay for training of child care workers, create resource and referral agencies, and provide grants for new child care services and to renovate existing centers.

Opponents of the legislation have called the proposal's $2.5 billion price tag too high. Actually that amount probably wouldn't even provide adequate services in a single state the size of California. Canada, far ahead of the United States in child care, recently passed an additional $5.4 billion child care bill. It will take an infusion of money and national leadership to expand and improve our child care services. The reason the price is so high is that we have waited too long to tackle this job. We are paying for the consequences of our procrastination.

The bill that Sen. Orin Hatch, a conservative Republican, proposed was more limited, establishing a $250 million block grant program to increase child care services. States could award this money to local governments, small business groups, educational institutions, and nonprofit organizations for such projects as voucher programs and subsidies for low-income families, start-up costs for employer-sponsored child care, training programs, and temporary care for sick children. The bill would also establish a revolving loan fund of $25 million so that family day-care operators could bring their homes into compliance with their state licensing standards. Finally, the Hatch proposal includes several tax incentives for businesses, homemakers, and family day-care operators.

One of the major differences between the two approaches concerns whether or not the federal government should couple funding with adherence to standards. The ABC bill set federal standards for child care providers that the states must implement within five years. After that—no standards, no money. Senator Hatch, reflecting the prevailing attitude among conservatives, leaves standards to the states. I don't think basic safety requirements should vary from state to state. An unfenced yard on a busy street is just as dangerous to the three-year-old in Mississippi as it is to the three-year-old in Massachusetts. Children everywhere need fire escapes.

Moving beyond these particular bills, another key difference between the two sides in the child care debate lies in their approach to tax credits. Conservatives do not want tax benefits targeted to working parents. They feel that would be an incentive for women to work and would discriminate against women who choose to stay home. Actually, since the first tax code was passed in 1913, our policies have been geared to families in which the mother stays at home. The marriage penalty tax, Social Security discrimination, and limited child care deductions all penalize working women. If government tax policy had so much influence on the way we live our lives, most women would now be at home. The truth of the matter is that the economy, not government tax policy, has been the driving force behind the new influx of mothers into the workplace. With the huge debt we are running, tax credits for everyone would drain the Treasury, give extra money to those who don't need it, and fail to provide adequate help for those who do. Tax credits should be targeted to those who work.

Phyllis Schlafly and other conservatives assail comprehensive child care reform as "federal baby-sitting" and threaten that it will mean more children in centers and less parenting. The world has changed. Not many of America's families fit Schlafly's model. We need more than a 7- to 10-percent solution! If we provide quality day care, we relieve people of a serious problem and help them be much better parents. That should be our goal.

President Ronald Reagan, in proclaiming the National Child Care Awareness Week of 1988, issued a statement about child care that reflects the conservatives' view (and is also like saying the highway program must recognize people who don't drive). He said, "To be fair to all families, child care policy analysis must recognize the contributions of women who work, those who prefer to work part-time rather than full-time jobs, and homemakers who forgo employment income altogether to raise children at home."[13]

That was a great plan—if the money could have been found. But let's be clear. Conservatives have found only words so far. They have not offered *any* policies that add substance to these platitudes. They have not taken any steps to make part-time work a more attractive alternative for employers and employees. They fight bills that do so. They have not pushed for a higher personal tax exemption that would help all people with children. They do nothing for the first category—"women who work."

No one calling for child care assistance is advocating that government take over the functions of parents. Parents, by seeking help, aren't abdicating their roles. To suggest that only increases the guilt of already guilt-prone people. The hardest thing for a mother or father to do is to ask for help—it was for me. Parents are supposed to have everything under control. Families want to be self-sufficient and they want to take good care of their children. Government should understand the changes and stresses people are experiencing and do everything possible to make it easier for parents to ask for help.

We need to unleash American know-how on the child care crisis. Parents, business, and government must be creative. We should provide incentives to business to come up with child care solutions. Senator Hatch's proposal of allowing employers to write off 25 percent of the expenses of establishing on-site or near-site child care centers is a good start.

One powerful resource is our older citizens, who should be given part-time job opportunities to work at child care centers. Seniors are an untapped labor pool. Many older people welcome extra income, enjoy children, and can greatly enrich the lives of the kids. Rep. Frank Guarini of New Jersey and I have introduced legislation that would earmark money, in the Older Americans Act, to hire seniors to work in child care centers, thus helping to reinforce intergenerational bonds. Gerontologists and child development experts agree that having older people care for our young is mutually beneficial.

I found from personal experience that everyone can profit from this type of arrangement. When I had Scott, my parents were living in Iowa and I didn't have any family around as a backup support system. Scott was a colicky baby and kept both Jim and me up for nights at a time. When we tried to get help, the pediatrician tried to cheer us up by pointing out that Albert Einstein only slept four hours a night. The trouble was he could never answer my question: "Do you know what happened to his mother?"

Because I had to do something to get Jim and me some sleep, I walked around the neighborhood and investigated who lived there. I found the Windolphs, a retired couple down the block, who immediately took to Scott. When we asked if they wanted a surrogate grandson one night a week, they loved the idea and offered to lend us a hand whenever we were in a bind. The arrangement worked out well. Scott got to be with other people who cared about him, our neighbors got to experience the joys of having a baby around the house, and we got to sleep.

What I have heard from my constituents and from families around the country—as well as my personal experiences with child care, part-time work, and other flexible work arrangements—has convinced me that parents can come up with their own formulas for their own particular circumstances. However, the government and the workplace have to give them the choices and the leeway and support they need. If we are going to enter the next century with a productive work force and strong family units, we have to get busy. Young people now look around them and wonder how they will ever manage to raise a family. The pressures of job and home seem overwhelming. Yet America is a nation whose strength derives from the home base, from family life. We must work to keep it that way.

6

Changing Life Cycles: Homemaking and the Displaced Housewife

WITHOUT fail, every year, some organization has a new idea for a cookbook and asks me to contribute a favorite recipe. I have to laugh because I really don't prepare meals beyond the hunt-and-gather stage. My "cookbook" consists of a list of the phone numbers of every carry-out restaurant within a fifteen-minute radius of my house. When people insist on a recipe, here's the one I send for breakfast: "Find a bowl. If it's on the floor, wash it because the dog was probably using it last. Find a box of cereal, preferably sugar-coated so you won't have to find the sugar. Find the milk but check the spoil date before pouring. Then assemble."

Even when I was growing up, I never had any particularly domestic inclination. I ate to live rather than lived to eat. I paid scant attention to food other than chocolate, even if it gave me a face on which people could play "connect the dots"! To this day, my favorite lunch is a large container of chocolate frozen yogurt from the House cafeteria.

The kitchen was always foreign territory to me and luckily, my lack of interest didn't bother my mother. Rather than force my hand, she found other chores for me to do. Dad didn't mind either and never sought to impose different standards on me and my brother just because I was a girl. Dad was of prairie-populist stock and believed that the brains in the family came from his mother's side of the family. My grandmother had been a real frontier woman, a scrapper and survivor who came West with her family in a covered wagon after her father left the whaling industry in Nantucket. Dad also loved to tell stories about his sister, Myrna, who, when they were young, was an ace with a bow and arrow. She never passed up a challenge to test her marksmanship, even with my dad's friends. Once, when she was begging to go along on a hunting trip with my father and his college buddies, they didn't want to take her but finally told her she could go if she could beat them with a bow and arrow. They had picked the wrong test. One by one the boys stepped into position, notched their arrows in place, and lifted their bows to aim for the target. The only bull's-eye belonged to my aunt, and the kid sister got to go.

Though I was raised in that tradition of independent women, it wasn't until I went to college in 1958 that I began to think seriously about my future. I wanted to be a ballerina, but Dad took home movies of my movements and when I saw them, I decided I lacked the talent. After high school I went to the University of Minnesota, an important experience both because I was on my own for the first time and because of the atmosphere on campus. Many of the students were the first in their families ever to go to college. For them, opportunities seemed limitless. They were living the American dream.

There were other changes, too. A quiet shift away from the conservatism of the postwar Midwest was beginning to take place. The civil rights movement was burgeoning and Sen. Hubert Humphrey drew huge crowds when he spoke on campus. He fired our imaginations with talk of racial and economic justice. When, as Senate majority leader, he was able to shepherd through the Congress important civil rights legislation, I felt that anything was possible and that I could be a part of it.

My class at the university was made up almost equally of men and women. The women felt they belonged and competed for achievement alongside the male students. (The university even allowed me to fly its ROTC planes—if I paid.) Though equality came early to the university, I don't think that all the women sat around, as I did, dreaming of going to China and studying Chinese. In my sorority, Chi Omega, many of the girls paid more attention to finding a husband than they did to studying. None of us gave much thought to how we would manage after we graduated. Would we be full-time homemakers? That was taken for granted. Even though we may have had career plans, few challenged that destiny. After college we would work, get married, and keep working until the first child was born. Then we would stay home and maybe go back later.

For as long as I can remember, I had wanted to go to law school. I think I saw it as a way of going up against the status quo. Applying to Harvard Law School only heightened the challenge. My father had planned to go to law school before the Depression and had dreamed about going to Harvard. Money, or the complete lack of it, got in his way. Although I wasn't aware of it at the time, I'm sure that at some point I became his hope for fulfilling that dream.

Being married and going to school at the same time gave Jim and me a chance to get used to life as a "two-learner" couple. When we moved to Denver we both worked, but those first years as a dual-career couple certainly didn't prepare me for what was to come. When I began to stay at home with my son it was a shock to learn that I didn't like being a full-time homemaker. The truth is, I failed homemaking. I found it incredibly frustrating. I was generating all kinds of busywork for myself. I was never one to wax the driveway or anything else. People who love to do the white-glove test and announce, "Oh, how wonderful! All the tops of the doorframes have been dusted," didn't do it for me! I kept trying, but I found the struggle for impeccably neat closets and dresser drawers exasperating. I was turning into a martyr. I didn't like it and nobody around me did either.

It was a time of sorting things out. I had to grapple with my own ambition and what, in spite of my rather unorthodox upbringing, I was conditioned to believe was expected of a new mother. It was as difficult a question then as it is now. How do you manage it all? In some ways I was lucky: I had a tolerant family and a husband who supported my decision to practice law, to teach, and to raise children, all at the same time.

Despite the glorification of homemaking for several decades, the American family has functioned, historically, as both an economic *and* a social unit. The concept is in our language: Ma-and-Pa store, farm ranch . . . The words acknowledge the dual roles men and women have as providers *and* parents. The husband and wife were economic *and* family partners.

What happened? In the 1950s, after World War II, this country redefined the roles. The father was mainly the provider and the mother mainly the parent. Suburbs began to ring our cities. If a man walked down the street of a suburb during the day, folks might call the police. These communities were daylight female ghettos, and though it was a new phenomenon, we said, "This is how it's always been."

In the mid-1960s and early 1970s, more women were graduating from college, entering the work force, going to graduate school, and returning to outside jobs after having children than at any other time in history. The civil rights movement had created a broad-based movement for equality that women could identify with on their own behalf. Many women began publicly to question their assigned role as homemaker only. They began to speak out against barriers to opportunity wherever they found them, in the university, in the workplace, and in marriage.

Sex roles came under the close scrutiny of a host of observers. Psychologists, sociologists, lawyers, and other experts questioned the inequality in marriage, and the most radical among them dismissed the family on the grounds that it was a hierarchic and patriarchal institution that had outlived its usefulness. Others fretted about the increasing divorce rate and about a new hedonism. For several years, commentators had a field day fighting among themselves about what was wrong. From their point of view, the family looked more like a battlefield than a haven.

But in reality, despite the growing debate over its future, most Americans believed in the family as our basic institution. The statistics for divorce were high and on the increase, but so were the figures for remarriage. The majority of Americans who divorced did not give up on marriage, they just went looking for a more perfect union. People did not stop having children, they tried to figure out the best way to manage.[1]

Conservatives reacted to the discussion about familial roles by taking the position that the only thing wrong with the family and homemaking was their critics. They argued that the family was fine as long as it was left alone. They fought for what one historian called "a mythic past of male individualism and female domesticity." They didn't acknowledge the social and economic changes that had altered the reality of most couples' lives. Instead, they called for a return to "traditional" values and roles. What that meant was, quite simply, women at home, probably in the suburbs, and men on the job. That this was no longer possible, or necessarily desirable, was not to be considered. That the fifties definition of marriage was unfair to both women *and* men was made to seem a radical idea. The Ozzie-and-Harriet marriage was the only valid kind and must be preserved forever.

There were, however, champions on the other side. Policymakers, spurred on by the women's movement and the increasing number of women entering the work force, became concerned about the effects of sexual discrimination. A handful of pioneers pushed Congress to act to correct the social and economic injustices women faced. The most ambitious of their plans was a proposal to amend the Constitution to specifically guarantee women's rights. The Equal Rights Amendment (ERA) first came to the Congress in 1923, amazing though that seems. Then, year after year, it was introduced, fought over, dropped. Frequently it was introduced, referred to committee, and ignored altogether. In fact, it languished in the House Judiciary Committee until August 1970, when Rep. Martha Griffiths, an eight-term Democrat from Michigan, forced a vote with a successful petition to discharge the Judiciary Committee from further consideration of the Equal Rights Amendment. In other words, they were no longer able to sit on the proposal. The following session, Congresswoman Griffiths succeeded in securing the first congressional approval for the amendment.[2]

That same year, Rep. Edith Green, a Democrat from Oregon, held hearings on discrimination against women in education. Out of those hearings came one of the most important antidiscrimination laws, Title IX of the Education Amendment of 1972. This statute prohibits discrimination on the basis of sex in any education program that receives federal funds. Without Title IX we would never have had as many female Olympic gold medal winners as we've achieved in recent years, because a "jockocracy" controlled school and university athletic programs.

As you can see, I arrived in Congress during an exciting time for women. The fight for state ratification of the ERA had just begun. It was on the ballot in my state when I was elected, and it passed. I jumped right into the fray, speaking on the amendment whenever I could, even though in some quarters it was a most unpopular idea.

The ERA was a clear constitutional mandate that men and women be treated equally at all levels of government. After all, governments tax men and women equally! Some people thought we had already achieved this goal and did not need a constitutional amendment. I did not agree. I believed the Equal Rights Amendment was necessary because discrimination against individuals based on sex is deeply entrenched in our laws and persistently reflected in governmental action. Further, even if specific laws were passed for women, they could be repealed. A constitutional mandate is a much more solid foundation for legal equality than are individual laws. For example, while, historically and actually, marriage is both an economic and a social partnership, the laws governing the institution defined married women as second-class citizens. The U.S. Commission on Civil Rights put it this way: "State laws set different rules for males and females entering marriage, define different rights for them during marriage with respect to property, to each other, to their children, and to third parties, and grant different rights at the end of marriage."[3]

Conservatives like Phyllis Schlafly took the lead against the ERA, painting a distorted picture of the social consequences of the amendment. She and others claimed it would mandate everything from unisex toilets to forced military service for women. But their main objective seemed to be to reinforce women's traditional role within marriage. Schlafly argued that the ERA, by eliminating a woman's dependence on her husband and his "duty" to support her, would destroy the family. In her 1972 report, she twisted the idea of equality into an absurd proportion. "The laws of every one of the 50 states now require the husband to support his wife and children. . . . The Equal Rights Amendment will remove this sole obligation from the husband, and make the wife equally responsible to provide a home for her family, and to provide 50 percent of the financial support." (The ERA has never passed, so women must be very well-off because husbands must support them, according to Schlafly!)

I debated Phyllis Schlafly once on ABC television during my first few months in Congress. It was unpleasant, start to finish. I arrived a little early after rushing with the kids and Jim to church and McDonald's, our usual Sunday-morning activities. I was going over some notes when Schlafly arrived with her entourage of "lieutenants" surrounding her as if she were the shah of Iran. Two of them came up to me as if to look me over and began telling me how wonderful Phyllis was, how she could do anything. Then, as they turned to leave to catch up with their fearless leader, one of them commented loudly, "She isn't bad-looking for a placard-carrying freak." I could not fathom what type of people these women were.

The television program was very frustrating. Schlafly had a peculiar way of disarming the moderator—she sounded like a lawyer, yet her fluffy feminine attire and artificially sweet voice kept him from treating her like one. She would take things out of context, distort the effects of the amendment, and call ERA proponents man-haters and Communists. Schlafly was never asked to explain why she opposed the ERA even though she herself was a professional career woman who had graduated from law school, run for Congress, and become a regular on the national lecture circuit. She took advantage of all the gains in equality won by our foremothers without ever saying thank you! Indeed, Phyllis Schlafly had become a model career woman in every way except her rhetoric. Her new career, apparently, was to be sure no one followed in her footsteps. Even I have probably cooked more meals at home than she has.

From the beginning, Schlafly argued that the ERA was for working women only and that it would be disastrous for homemakers if passed. She pronounced herself the champion of homemakers and accused ERA advocates of being against motherhood. She claimed that we opposed marriage. Her proof? We talked about rights for women in the workplace, educational opportunities for women, and the unequal treatment women received in divorce. She dismissed the argument that divorced homemakers had any rights. To Schlafly, a woman had all the protection she needed in her husband. If she wanted to keep her rights, she shouldn't be getting a divorce. In Schlafly's world view, you were either in favor of the traditional family or you weren't for the family at all. You certainly couldn't be pro-family and at the same time want to improve women's lives. I was amused the morning after the debate when I got a call from Jill Ruckelshaus at the White House, a Republican. She wanted to know if they could trade Schlafly to the Democratic party. I told her, "No thanks!"

What Schlafly and the conservatives chose to ignore then, and still do, was that the nature of the family had already changed. All she had to do was look at the lives women actually were leading. They were significantly different from those of their mothers and grandmothers. Young women were better educated and had higher levels of work experience. For these reasons, among others, they had to combine a variety of new roles in their lives and at work. They were being asked to help provide care for elderly parents at a time when they were still caring for young children. And though no one was overjoyed at the prospect, there were more single-parent families headed by mothers. More people were getting divorced, including a growing number of mid-life women who had followed Schlafly's advice and been full-time homemakers. She did not care about their plight. I guess she felt that if they had been good homemakers, they would not be divorced.

By the early 1980s, the majority of Americans supported efforts to pass the Equal Rights Amendment, but that majority has not been translated into victory because of the complexities of the state ratification system. Though the conservatives may have won the battle on the ERA, at least temporarily, they have lost the war. They haven't kept women out of the work force, and as for all the talk, that's all it was. They have done nothing to improve family life or the situation of the homemaker. Homemakers themselves have emerged as their own advocates.

The details of some of these issues were new to me when I first got to Congress and I had to educate myself on what was happening. For example, I didn't know much about divorce from personal experience when I arrived in Washington. No one in my immediate family had been divorced, and I didn't practice much family law as an attorney. But within a short time it became evident to me that a domestic crisis had erupted in this country. (The rate of divorce has, I'm happy to say, declined somewhat in the 1980s.) In 1975, the increasing number of divorces in long-term marriages gave rise to the Alliance for Displaced Homemakers, a self-help, grass-roots advocacy organization that numbers between two and three million women and speaks for an estimated fifteen million. These women were victims of the quiet transformation in the structure of the American family.[4]

I met with Tish Sommers and Laurie Shields, founders of the Alliance for Displaced Homemakers, who described the plight of women who had agreed to a specific social contract: man as breadwinner, woman as homemaker. They had assumed that benefits like health insurance and economic security flowed from their *marriage*. Both Tish and Laurie learned otherwise when one was divorced and the other was widowed in her mid-fifties. Tish Sommers learned that she would not be eligible for Social Security or standard Medicare at sixty-five because she was older than her ex-husband and would have to wait until he reached retirement age. Laurie Shields found that her job credentials were essentially worthless because she'd worked only at home for twenty years. For the latter reason, neither woman was eligible for unemployment insurance. They fell through the cracks of all available programs because they were too young for assistance for the elderly and too old to have well-paying careers of their own. Legally they were treated as throw-aways.[5]

They, and the primarily mid-life women they represent, had been exiled from a role, an occupation, and a livelihood. When they formed the Alliance for Displaced Homemakers, such women were not active feminists. They were forced to become advocates on their own behalf, and while they were doing it, they helped create the ideas and language that would eventually assist policymakers trying to work for reform. The heart of the matter was: society has to learn to recognize homemaking as valuable labor, and marriage as an economic partnership, legally as well as rhetorically. Yet the very people who said they were supporters of the "traditional" family fought against the legal protection of women who had followed their advice and spent their lives as homemakers.

Change was slow, but it did begin. In the 1970s, the introduction of no-fault divorce laws in many states lessened the stigma attached to being divorced by making the process easier and less demeaning. In those states, a husband or wife no longer had to have grounds for divorce and couples didn't have to go through the wrenching experience of proving adultery, mental cruelty, or desertion, the only grounds for divorce in many states. But as harsh as the traditional divorce laws were, as Lenore Weitzman has pointed out in her book, *The Divorce Revolution,* the old laws did uphold the conventional roles and responsibilities in marriage.[6] A wife suing for spousal support based on her contribution as a homemaker could bargain effectively for a greater share of the assets when her husband was at fault.

Although the new laws brought a degree of justice and equity to the divorce process, the court settlements did just the opposite. The economic reality for women and their children under the new laws often was financial disaster. In recent years divorced women and their children have experienced a 73 percent drop in income and in their standard of living in the first year, while their husbands enjoyed a 42 percent rise in theirs.[7] In other words, "no-fault" often resulted in economic punishment for women and children.

What the courts overlooked are the economic inequalities created during a "traditional" marriage. Judges ignored the contributions of a homemaker to the marriage, the children's care, and her husband's career. They also failed to consider that the husband held the major assets of the marriage: his salary, pension, health insurance, and potential long-term earning power. Marriage was considered a partnership, but it was not, because one partner had no access to the assets of the company. By the very nature of her work the wife was hampered from making money on her own. Courts rarely took into account the lack of earning capacity of the long-term homemaker who no longer had marketable skills.

In 1975, Congress began to turn its attention to the problems of displaced homemakers. The Committee on Education and Labor held the first hearings on the economic barriers mid-life and older women faced. Congress also undertook the first study of women and Social Security. By the following year, amid a growing number of studies and hearings on mid-life women, Congress authorized federal grants for school-based counselors to assist women reentering school and appropriated money to improve the accessibility of vocational education to displaced home-makers.

Two years later, Congress expanded the newly created Comprehensive Employment and Training Act (CETA) to include a displaced-homemakers program to train middle-aged or older women to reenter the work force and to help prepare women who had never worked for entry into the labor force. This was a very important victory, but unfortunately, it reached only a limited number of women.

There were many hearings and studies in the seventies on the treatment of women under the retirement system, Social Security, and the tax code. Hearings on mothers' participation in the labor force, sex discrimination in employment, and the problems of the elderly demonstrated just how extensive and complex the problem was.

In about 1975, I began to get letters from the widows and divorced wives of civil servants, members of the military and the foreign service, CIA officers, and railroad retirees. These women sent pages and pages of documents, from their marriage certificates to their court orders, or the death certificates of their husbands. They wanted to know why after twenty or thirty years of marriage they had no pension, no Social Security, no health insurance. These were proud women who had committed their lives to homemaking, to being career military, foreign service, CIA, civil service, or railroad wives. Now they were left impoverished, or close to it, because of divorce or widowhood. They wrote me because they thought that, as a woman, I might be sympathetic to their situation and because they didn't know where else to go.

As part of my work on the Armed Services Committee, I traveled from base to base in this country and overseas. On these trips I met with military and foreign service wives who made a very deep impression on me. Because my own family had moved so much when I was a child I could understand the hardships these women suffered when they had to move somewhere new every few years. They were dedicated to their marriages, but they were angry that neither the State Department nor the Pentagon recognized the contribution they made to the national effort or seemed to care about what happened to them after the many years of unpaid service they gave.

The foreign service wives were very well organized. In 1976, the Association of American Foreign Service Women (AAFSW) sent out a worldwide survey on a variety of topics, including one of particular concern—women facing divorce after long marriages and long "careers" as wives in the foreign service.

What they found was alarming. Wives were left, after long years of unpaid government service abroad, with no employment record, no modern skills, no Social Security, no shared annuity, no survivor benefits, and no group medical insurance. In addition, since only 14 percent of divorced women nationally were awarded alimony or spousal support at that time, foreign service wives were going into retirement with meager or no resources. There were, at the time, ambassadors' former wives who were working as cleaning ladies.

Perhaps nothing illustrated the situation as dramatically as the life of Jane Dubbs, former wife of the U.S. ambassador to Afghanistan. Jane had been divorced and had returned to the United States. Then, on May 28, 1979, her former husband of thirty years was assassinated in Afghanistan. His death was a tragedy and it also made Jane a pauper. Her alimony payments stopped, she wasn't entitled to Social Security, and the ambassador's death benefits and an estimated $20,000-a-year pension went to his second wife, to whom he had been married for only three years.

It all seemed particularly unfair because, until 1972, foreign service spouses were graded and their performance had an effect on their husbands' careers. Women like Jane were expected to entertain, organize social functions, and attend to other official and unofficial duties, volunteering their time to the foreign service community while continuing to tend to their own families' welfare. The State Department got, and expected, "two for the price of one."

In 1972, the State Department finally declared that spouses were no longer to be treated as associate employees of the department; their contributions would no longer be mentioned in employees' personnel files or efficiency reports. But the new policy did not deal effectively with reality. The State Department did not hire anyone else to fill the wife's "voluntary" functions. The tradition of service continued, and the lack of recompense or benefits also continued. As one former foreign service wife testified: "The emancipation proclamation does not work. The wife is still an unpaid and unappreciated employee of the Department of State." Jane Dubbs explained, "All those years in the foreign service I thought I *had* a job and was entitled to something." But Dubbs, after serving with her husband for thirty years—and his career advanced partly because of her services—had no prospect of a job, no annuity, no health insurance.

One wife described her time in the foreign service to me as "life among the packing crates." In addition to the turmoil of moving homes and families to new and sometimes frightening environments, foreign service families faced special problems: culture shock, language barriers and isolation, disruptions in schooling for children, exotic medical problems, and difficulty maintaining adequate health and hygiene for the family. Wives were also discouraged or even prohibited from working in most of the foreign countries they were assigned to.

Though several cosmetic changes were made by the State Department, it was clear that it would take an act of Congress to redress the situation of the former spouses of foreign service employees. In 1977, I introduced several former spouse bills, one each for the foreign service, the military, the civil service, and the CIA. Separate bills were necessary because each service has its own federal retirement system and is governed by its own unique set of laws. I moved forward in these four areas because

I thought fairness and equity gave me a real chance to win: these bills followed a standard already available to the general population in many states. State courts often divided private pensions on the premise that marriage is an economic partnership. In view of the additional duties imposed on wives of federal employees, the federal government had a special responsibility to catch up with this practice.

We had been giving these women the message that society expected them to remain in the home, care for their families, and further their husbands' careers. If they followed those instructions and then something happened to the marriage, we abandoned them. The legislation I proposed mandated that state courts automatically provide a pro rata share of the annuity and survivor benefits to the former wife. Her share would be based on a formula using the number of years of marriage during a husband's career at the time of divorce. The reason for an automatic division was simple: it would ensure that all spouses were treated the same and that they would not have to pursue a costly court fight to win what was theirs to begin with. This provision went further than state laws: state courts had been free to do what they wished in the area of private pensions and annuities, and they were forbidden to divide federal pensions. Uniform treatment of federal pensions would eliminate the inequities that existed from state to state and court to court and would make it impossible for people in federal service to "forum shop" and proceed with divorce in a state that didn't divide pensions.

There already was precedent for my bills in the Social Security system. Congress permitted a wife who had been married for twenty years at the time of divorce to be eligible for Social Security benefits on the basis of her former husband's earning record. In 1977, Congress took an important leap forward and reduced the marriage requirement to ten years, effective in 1979. The Social Security Amendment of 1977 also increased benefits for a widow who remarries after age sixty from one half of her husband's pension to the full amount.

Building on this Social Security victory was not easy. Each battle had to be fought and won independently. We moved first on the civil service pension and immediately ran into strong opposition from House members on my own committee. Members of Congress receive federal pensions themselves, so we weren't just debating the issue of whether a pension should be divided between any husband and wife, but whether these men believed *their* wives should have any right to a share of *their* pension. One powerful member of the committee, who had already been married two or three times, was dead set against the bill and had many powerful allies.

The committee voted down my bill and accepted a compromise: as part of divorce settlements, state courts could decide how to divide civil service pensions, and the Office of Personnel Management would have to honor court orders that awarded a share of a pension to a former spouse. It was not what I had hoped for, but at least the federal pension was no longer beyond the law. The committee rejected the former spouse's right to survivor benefits, a great loss. It took six more years and much hard work until we finally passed legislation authorizing state courts also to divide survivor annuities, extend medical benefits to former spouses, and grant annuities to certain long-term former spouses who were left out of the law.

The opposition I ran into on the Civil Service Committee was similar to what I found in the Armed Services Committee and the Department of Defense. Members of the armed services railed against the bill in the most vitriolic fashion. One retired officer summed it all up when he said, "We reject out of hand that the wife contributed to the earning of retirement benefits. There are few wives who participated in the fighting, separation, the risks and dangers and assignments."

We tried unsuccessfully for close to four years to get a pro rata division of military pensions. The Supreme Court had a lot to do with our problems. In 1979, in *Hisquierdo v. Hisquierdo* (439 U.S. 572), the Court had held that federal pensions for railroad retirees could not be divided at the time of divorce and that the state courts had no jurisdiction over them. And then, to set things back even further, in 1981, in *McCarty v. McCarty* (453 U.S. 210), the Supreme Court reaffirmed that under present law state courts could not divide military retirement pay or pensions. The only good news was that the Court did not necessarily endorse the ruling's social impact. In fact, Justice Harry A. Blackmun, writing for the majority, virtually invited Congress to consider a change in the law to allow such a division to be made:

> We recognize that the plight of an ex-spouse of a retired service member is often a serious one. . . . Congress may well decide, as it has in the Civil Service and Foreign Service contexts, that more protection should be afforded a former spouse of a retired service member. The decision, however, is for Congress alone.

The McCarty decision galvanized former-spouse groups to lobby Congress to overturn the Supreme Court decision. By September 1982, the Uniformed Services Former Spouses' Protection Act (FSPA) was enacted into law, returning to the states the authority to divide military pensions and to order direct payment to former spouses married at least ten years. The legislation also permitted a retiree to name a former spouse as beneficiary of a survivor annuity.

Overturning the effects of McCarty was a limited victory, but we hoped we could build on it. The hearing record for FSPA supported our view that military life placed unique demands and hardships on spouses. Congress recognized that the spouse is a partner in the member's career from the time the couple enters the military. We learned that wives are expected to fill an important role in the social life and welfare of the military community and that the military, in fact, exerts pressure on wives to volunteer their time to the military community. Child care and management of the family household are frequently solely the wife's responsibility. She must endure long separations from her husband and undertake frequent moves—on the average, every three years. Because of the demands of military life, there are special pressures on the wife to be a homemaker. It is difficult, if not impossible, for her to pursue a career of her own.

As it turned out, in some states, the Former Spouses' Protection Act was no protection at all. Shortly after the bill was enacted into law, the attorney general of Virginia, Gerald L. Baliles, who would later become governor, said that Virginia courts would not regard pensions as property.[8] Obviously, military personnel looking for a divorce forum flocked to Virginia, where former wives were locked out of their ex-husbands' pensions. One former spouse, who raised three children and gave up a library job to go with her husband to Portugal, told me, "Congress is still saying that if he goes out and earns the money, then I don't share in it, and that we who stay home taking care of children . . . don't have a right to share in his pension either. Then all you are is a glorified housekeeper, not a marriage partner."

Elizabeth June Meyers found this out the hard way when her husband divorced her against her wishes after she'd been a military wife for thirty-five years. She had raised five sons as her husband rose through the ranks to become a captain in the Navy. During that time, she had enjoyed the privileges that position conferred upon them, but when she was divorced, Mrs. Meyers no longer had free medical care, she was barred from shopping at the base commissary, and she had no interest in her ex-husband's military pension or, in the event of his death, in his survivor benefits. All those benefits were made available to his second wife, even though their marriage lasted only thirty-nine days. There were thousands of cases like this. Women who never thought they'd be pushing for women's rights were now some of the country's greatest activists.

As sad and outrageous as the experiences of these ex-wives were, the letters I received from them helped me keep up the fight. I was spurred on also every time one of the military brass would pull me aside and tell me to stop interfering in the private lives of his soldiers. These men were still in the Dark Ages. One lieutenant colonel complained that merely returning authority to the states to divide pensions went too far: "They're [former spouses] getting something they didn't earn. A wife may be deserving of income and support, but military retirement pay is reduced current compensation for reduced current service." He then added somewhat maliciously, "A woman with a tear in her eyes can get more than a man with his arms and legs shot off."[9] I was amazed that men like this felt they should have special privileges and be above the state laws everyone else had to obey.

Though we have a long way to go, we've made some important gains. Former military spouses are now entitled to continued health benefits, an equal voice in choosing to participate in the Survivor Benefit Plan when they are married, and the survivor annuity as part of the divorce settlement.

There was one other bright moment in the fight to achieve pension rights for homemakers. In 1980, after a bitter fight, Congress finally acknowledged that divorced foreign service spouses had an earned right to retirement and survivor benefits. The foreign service wives persuaded members of Congress to recognize their contributions to their marriages, to their husbands, and to the foreign service. Many members voted in favor of the controversial amendment because they argued that the foreign service wives faced hardships other wives didn't face. They were especially sympathetic because foreign service wives were not entitled to Social Security. Whatever the reason, Congress had in this special instance validated marriage as an economic partnership.

In 1982, we took up the effort again, this time on behalf of CIA spouses. It is interesting to remember that these women wrote to William Casey, then head of the CIA, and to former directors and/or their wives, for help in changing the law. Mr. Casey responded that his hands were tied until changes were made by Congress. Obviously he was not an advocate! However, William Colby, CIA director under Nixon, did become an advocate and volunteered his services as legal advisor.

Even though Congress had established a pension and annuity right for former foreign service spouses, the CIA wives found they had to revisit many of the same arguments and debates. CIA spouses faced additional challenges because of the double roles that resulted from their husbands' cover assignments and simultaneous employment as CIA covert officers. They also had to deal with the stress of their husbands' dangerous assignments, the loneliness and fear of being by themselves with a family in a foreign country without diplomatic support, and in some cases extremely hazardous conditions such as terrorism and bombings.

None of this seemed to move the members of the House Intelligence Committee until CIA spouses gave them a warning during their testimony: without the right to a government annuity of their own at the time of divorce, they would be forced to reveal their husbands' occupation in divorce proceedings. Otherwise, they said, the judges would be ill-informed and treat them unfairly!

I was able to help the legislation through Congress, but the real credit goes to the spouses who won the fight when in 1982, and again in 1984, legislation was passed giving CIA spouses a pro rata share of retirement and survivor benefits if the marriage ended in divorce.

Private pensions weren't perfect either. By the early 1980s, the pump for pension reform had been sufficiently primed so that women could take on the private sector and confront the inequities for homemakers under the Employee Retirement Income Security Act. Rep. Geraldine Ferraro took the lead and, with the help of a broad range of women's organizations who had developed their own pension experts, began the push to pass the Retirement Equity Act (REA). The legislation aimed to strengthen the pension rights of both homemakers and women who entered the work force. In 1983, when the bill was first introduced, one half of all women were full-time homemakers. At about that time, less than 11 percent of women over sixty-five received private pensions and annuities, compared with nearly 28 percent of men over sixty-five.[10]

Pension plans have rewarded the long-term steady worker who has low mobility and high earnings. Even if a woman spent some part of her adult life working outside the home, she was often not vested in a pension plan because of her irregular work pattern or her low-paying job. For example, a woman who left the work-place when her children were born usually did so early in her work career, and if she returned to work when the children started school, she often took a part-time job that rarely provided pension benefits. Even a homemaker who expected to share in her husband's pension, and to receive survivor benefits upon his death, often discovered at the funeral that she wasn't provided for because her husband had "opted out." Before REA passed, husbands could unilaterally decide to forgo survivor benefits in favor of a higher monthly pension check. As surprising as it may seem, in 1981, over 60 percent of husbands did opt out and left widows with no survivor annuity whatsoever.

Sometimes husbands unwittingly left wives with nothing. If a husband died before retiring, even though he had become fully vested in his pension plan, his wife often would not be entitled to receive any benefits. Under many plans at the time, no matter how long he'd worked, a husband who died even just a few days short of retirement left his wife with nothing.

A divorced homemaker had a rough time trying to collect a share of her husband's pension even when the court awarded it to her. Many plans refused to pay these women because they claimed that national legislation made it impossible to make payments from the pension to anyone other than the pensioner. Despite numerous court decisions ruling that this interpretation was incorrect—Congress intended to protect workers only from their creditors, not to shield them from family responsibilities—divorced spouses still had difficulty collecting their money.

The passage of the REA in 1984 was a major breakthrough in pension equity and went a long way toward alleviating women's problems in this area. The law required the written consent of the spouse before the joint and survivor annuity could be waived by the worker. REA also assured that survivor benefits are paid to the spouse of any vested participant in a plan who dies before the age of retirement. It made clear to employers that divorced spouses who receive a court-ordered share of the pension are to be paid directly. Other pension reforms in the REA were made to accommodate women's irregular work patterns: the law lowered the age of participation and liberalized rules for working women who stayed out of the work force to have children.

The difference between 1977, when I introduced the first pension legislation, and 1984, when the REA passed, was marked. I think one of the most important reasons for this change was the work of the Congressional Caucus for Women's Issues. The caucus was initially organized in 1977, as the Congresswomen's Caucus, to give us a chance to discuss issues affecting women, to gather information, and to set up meetings with high-level Cabinet staff to discuss our agenda. In the early years, the caucus was open only to women members and was governed by consensus, a process that prevented us from being very effective and limited what we could accomplish.

The idea for the caucus grew out of an informal group I participated in from the time I arrived in 1973. The congresswomen used to reserve a table in the members' dining room and meet regularly during lunch to exchange information. In many ways it was an extension of the suburban "coffee-klatsch"; but in this situation it not only kept us in touch with each other, it gave us a chance to develop strategies for getting our legislation through Congress. We decided to make the group a formal entity because we thought we would be more powerful as a unified body. But it took time before we evolved into an effective legislative organization.

One of the main problems was that membership initially included all the congresswomen, and some of them did not want the caucus to do much, especially not to rock the boat. Conservative members were worried about being labeled feminists, and the feminists were afraid of being muzzled, so it was hard for us to agree on what to do. It was frustrating for me much of the time because I wanted to get things moving on a fast track. The Congresswomen's Caucus in its early form was more an ongoing tea party than a convincing legislative caucus.

But to be fair, the caucus did initiate some important projects, laying a solid foundation for our work later on. The data we collected on topics such as alimony, child support, and Small Business Administration loans helped identify the problems women faced and what needed to be done to remedy them. We had our own team of researchers looking into education, employment, and retirement equity for women. We also worked hard to push the Carter administration to evaluate the role of women in the government at every level.

By 1981, faced with a new administration that not only opposed the ERA but that sought to cut back programs we cared deeply about, those of us most involved in the caucus decided to reorganize. The first thing we did was to impose dues of $2,500 instead of the old $50. The money not only put the caucus on a par with other legislative service organizations, it was also a way to ensure a commitment from those members who joined. Not surprisingly, congresswomen who had been members in name only dropped out, leaving a core of more activist members. We then scrapped the consensus process for a more democratic one facilitated by the cochairs. Several months later we opened nonvoting membership to congressmen. We collected dues from them as well, though a smaller amount than what the women paid. The decision to open membership to men was a pragmatic one: with more allies and resources we could accomplish more. Even so, many of us felt it was important for the congresswomen to retain control of the caucus's leadership, and to do so we created an executive committee of women members.

I think probably the most significant thing to come out of the reorganization was a plan for the caucus to introduce each session an omnibus legislative package we called the Economic Equity Act (EEA). The EEA is made up of various bills with different congressional sponsors, all aimed at achieving a measure of economic equality for women. The components of the act are different each session because there are so many economic inequities for us to address. The EEA is one of the principal agendas for women in Congress, and for certain male members as well.

One of the caucus's most ambitious efforts grew out of concern over sex discrimination in the Social Security system. As we continued to look at the problems facing mid-life and older women, we discovered that at Social Security's inception in 1935, it was assumed there would be only one breadwinner in the family. In 1939, supplemental benefits were added for the worker's dependents—his wife and children. The system worked fairly well in the early years because at that time most families fit this traditional pattern and most couples stayed married. By the 1970s, however, the Social Security system no longer reflected the diversity of American lives and families. Especially, it was no longer responsive to the needs of American women.

A large part of the problem stems from the fact that earnings records are maintained for individual workers only, not for the family unit. Homemakers in the United States, unlike those in several other countries, do not receive Social Security credit for the years they spend raising children or caring for their families. Homemakers establish no earnings record of their own. A non-working spouse is entitled to a spousal benefit (also known as a dependent's benefit) equal to 50 percent of the worker's benefit. If the marriage survives into retirement, together the couple receives 150 percent of the husband's earned credits. But if the marriage ends in divorce, the homemaker is entitled to only one half of her husband's earned credits, *not* one half the combined amount they would receive if still married. A wife who moves in and out of the work force, or who works regularly but earns less than her husband, is treated as if she never worked. For example, a wife who works but then stays at home to bear children and raise a family obviously must have contributed to Social Security while in the work force. Nevertheless she is given a zero on her earnings record for every year after the first five she is out of the labor force. If she loses ten years of earnings because she is raising her family, she is not entitled to Social Security based on her own earnings. A homemaker is not entitled to disability benefits either if she has not participated in the labor force for five out of the ten years previous to her disability, and her family is not eligible for survivor benefits if she should die.

Although the Social Security system acknowledges that a wife has a right to a share of her husband's benefits at the time of divorce, if she divorces before she has been married ten years, she loses all earnings credit accumulated during her marriage except what she has earned on her own. A homemaker who left the work force for nine years to raise her children cannot qualify on her husband's earnings because she has not worked at a "paying" job during those years. It's a double bind. She doesn't have the money because she didn't work outside the home. She doesn't have the Social Security credit because she divorced after "only" nine years.

The caucus has backed reform efforts to implement an earnings sharing plan since its earliest days. It is a fundamental component of our legislative agenda in the EEA. Reps. Martha Keyes and Donald Fraser had pioneered the earnings sharing program in the seventies, and Rep. Mary Rose Oakar carried on the fight for implementing an earnings sharing plan in the eighties.

For Social Security purposes, under the caucus's plan, a couple's earnings would be added together rather than accounted separately, and that combined figure would appear on each spouse's earnings record. A spouse who left the labor force for homemaking and child-rearing would continue to receive earnings credits from the other spouse's income. When the homemaker reentered the labor force, his or her earnings would again be credited to the couple's total income. Thus the plan would provide both of them with Social Security protection based on labor-market work and unpaid work in the home.

In the case of divorce, a spouse would be entitled to half the earnings credits accumulated during the marriage; thus both the former spouses would have an earnings record on which to build after the divorce. Widows would inherit the total earnings credits accumulated by the couple during the marriage, thereby providing a higher Social Security benefit and more financial stability in later years.

Earnings sharing recognizes marriage as an interdependent economic partnership. This ideal is fundamental to the caucus's goals. Together with pension reform, earnings sharing underscored our efforts at making the economics of marriage more equitable. The reforms were not aimed at undermining marriage; rather they sought to close the gap between outmoded policies and the social, economic, and demographic realities of American society and the American family. By recognizing the value of homemaking, we believed we were letting families make their own choices. If a couple want to have one parent at home, neither the family nor the parent should be penalized financially. The fundamental principle at stake is economic equity. The fight to win parity under Social Security has been going on for well over a decade. We have not come close to winning, but we will continue the fight.

In 1981, shortly after the Reagan administration took office, the women in the caucus met with Social Security administrator John Svahn, to let him know of our concerns. We had been meeting with Cabinet members since 1977 to exchange views, but never had we been confronted with such arrogance as we were that day. We told the commissioner of the unequal treatment women, and especially wives, receive under Social Security. Although I don't remember his exact words, Svahn intimated that we didn't know what we were talking about. He kept repeating, "The Social Security system treats everyone the same." Rep. Lindy Boggs, a Democrat from Louisiana, who had come to the

House in 1973, leaned over and said to him, "Mr. Svahn, we have been looking at the problems mid-life women face for a long time. Our researchers have uncovered much disturbing evidence of unequal treatment under Social Security. I think you'd better look at the reports your own agency and others have issued over the last half dozen years before you go on talking." But Svahn was unmoved. Rep. Mary Rose Oakar tried again to get through. She explained to the commissioner the concept of earnings sharing, and how the previous administration had already done a superb job analyzing various scenarios to bring equality to Social Security. As an aside, hoping to give him a chance to come around, she told him that often it took a long time for a new concept to become a legislative reality, and that we were prepared to work with him to get earnings sharing implemented.

But it was clear that the commissioner hadn't come to listen. Rep. Margaret Heckler, a Republican from Massachusetts first elected in 1966, thanked the commissioner for attending the meeting and said that she too hoped we could work together with the administration on this problem. She reminded Mr. Svahn that we had been working for the last seven years and thought the time had come to push the legislation through Congress. But Svahn was undaunted by his fellow Republican and replied facetiously, "Well, I guess you've got another thirteen to go."

We tried again to reach the Reagan administration on these issues, this time through Mrs. Reagan. The congresswomen had a tradition of meeting with the First Lady every year to discuss issues concerning women and their families. We had some successes in the past in getting our concerns heard, but not this time. It took five months to arrange a luncheon with Mrs. Reagan and the vice president's wife, Mrs. Bush, and by May, when we finally met, the administration had already slashed half a dozen programs for women and children. We were afraid nothing would be left, especially because the administration was also reversing enforcement of existing programs, and undoing the gains that had been achieved.

We held the luncheon in one of the House dining rooms, but before we even began to eat, we knew it was hopeless. We had been told during the final arrangements that week that Mrs. Reagan would *not* discuss issues or anything to do with legislation. We thought she might be more flexible than her staff had indicated, but she stuck to her promise. I don't know what she thought we wanted to visit with her about. We were legislators and it was our business to pass laws. We had hoped that we could appeal to her as a woman and a mother as well as a public person, but Mrs. Reagan didn't seem to want to know what was going on. It really was a very sad and depressing moment, and it made us decide there was no reason to continue First Lady lunches in this administration.

When I think about my own goals in Congress, I realize that I have always tried to create opportunities by correcting inequalities. The caucus, which I cochair, has been really important in working toward that goal: if we get rid of the inequalities that hinder women, we strengthen the family at the same time. For me, building a family policy has meant finding a way to bridge the gap between public policy and the reality of women's lives. The conservatives' insistence that there is a contest between homemakers and working women is incorrect. Our legislation has made it possible for homemaking to be recognized and rewarded. We do not believe either in throw-away homemakers. We think America is a country that can recognize the needs of these women as well as those of women in the work force.

7

Affording the
American Dream

THE financial decisions we make each month, with pen and checkbook in hand, are heavily influenced by the health of the national economy. If the government is in financial trouble, chances are we feel the effects in the family budget. High inflation throughout the 1970s, coupled with back-to-back recessions in the early 1980s and the shift in federal priorities in the Reagan administration, have eroded family purchasing power. Many of us are having trouble providing what our parents did. Just as in previous generations, a house, an education for the children, a car, and health insurance are goals of the middle-class family, but they are now hard to attain. The fact is that the majority of families in this country, like the federal government itself, are living on borrowed money. Currently, 65 percent of American households are in debt and 55 percent *owe* more than they *own* in financial assets.[1]

I grew up in the aftermath of the Great Depression and my parents, like most who lived through the 1930s, passed on to us the value of thriftiness, resourcefulness, and just plain making-do. They would sit down with my brother and me to plan our vacation activities or to talk about what was needed by way of sharing chores and other family responsibilities. These responsibilities ran from cleaning our rooms to helping remodel wrecked airplanes, rebuild houses, or work in my father's insurance office during school vacations. Whatever was needed to help out, we were expected to do. We were never forced to work but were taught to see that working and doing chores was a responsibility we all shared. It's a lesson I've taken with me into my own life: don't worry about whose job it is or whether it's the right "status." Just get it done and move on to something that may be more fun.

When I was nine my parents decided it was time I learned about the real value of money and how fast it disappears. I was given an allowance meant to cover a month's worth of lunches, clothes, and anything else I might need. My mother thought it was important that we be given autonomy and responsibility early. My allowance looked like a huge sum to me at the beginning of each month and a paltry sum at the end. If I had no money left at the end of the month, all my parents said was "Tough." Eventually, through trial and error, I learned to budget my money to cover the basics, but for a long time my wardrobe was a hodgepodge "fad-of-the-week" collection.

My brother and I liked nothing better than to dream up innovative ways to make money. In high school we went into business buying, repairing, and selling job lots of damaged insurance salvage from mail-order houses. Later, we made annual trips to Detroit to bring year-old factory autos back to sell in Iowa, where the price was higher.

Watching my own children grow up in the 1970s and 1980s has been another education in economics. When I went into the Congress, it was clear that commuting between Denver and Washington meant we would have to keep two households going. It also meant that if I was to spend time with the kids, they would have to travel back and forth with me. There is no congressional allowance for family travel, and the result is that families are usually parked in one place and the member moves around. Jim and I decided early on that our top priority would be money for airfare, so that we could treat my job as a family seminar and be together as much as possible. We have managed, but only by giving up other things.

When the children were starting high school we walked them through the choices. We told them we could afford to send them to private school *or* we could continue to use the money we had for travel to Denver and for family vacations. We could not afford both. We also said if their grades were low, then there was no choice—they would have to go to private school. Luckily, this "bribery" system worked. Both Jamie and Scott wanted the mobility and so they studied without my constant nagging.

I was glad they chose to go to public high school for a lot of reasons, but that choice didn't stop them from wanting all the things that most teenagers want. Over the years I grew weary of hearing about designer clothes, hot cars, compact-disc players, and all sorts of other expensive things. I would get impatient until I remembered how I used to squander my own allowance and the lessons I learned from the way my family treated the problem. It is hard but very important to help children find a balance between what they can expect from us and what is their own responsibility.

Once, when Scott and Jamie were little, I overheard Scott telling his sister, "You always say you want something. You'll do much better if you say you need it." Obviously, he'd figured us out pretty early on.

Both children worked summers for pocket money. We helped them buy a car, though we practically had to refinance the house to keep up with the insurance premiums. Jamie, for all her intelligence, did not seem to pick up the finer points of driving, and she scraped and dented every car she drove. Instead of a visual system, she seemed to use a sonar system: if she heard a crunch she stopped.

Jamie did not go off to college until the year Scott graduated, so, fortunately, we did not have to pay tuition for two children at the same time. Even so, the cost of putting two children through eight consecutive years of a private university education is astronomical. Inflation has made tuition balloon, and housing and the other expenses associated with a college education are also sky-high. I couldn't be prouder that my children got into the schools they wanted, and I know we are fortunate to be able to absorb a lot of the expense without saddling them with a huge financial debt in the future. I want them to have as many choices open to them as possible. I know how deep the disappointment can be when you aren't able to afford to reach your dreams—as happened to my father when his family lost most of its money in the Depression.

As it turned out, the Great Depression played an important role in shaping how both my parents saw the role of government. The Depression had created an urgent need for government programs to help growing numbers of unemployed Americans find jobs, food, and shelter. My folks were actually luckier than many people at that time because they grew up on farms in Nebraska and their families were able to eke out an existence on the land. No one lived especially well, but they had enough food and were able to hold on to their farms. The government experimented with dozens of programs to get the country on its feet again, including agricultural programs to help farmers like my grandparents. One program, the Agriculture Adjustment Act of 1933, paid farmers to keep some of their fields out of cultivation in an effort to raise plummeting food prices and hold off the growing number of foreclosures. It wasn't surprising that both my parents became devoted to FDR for his efforts. Not everything he did worked, but he cared and he kept trying.

The innovative New Deal programs did not seem radical or outside of the American tradition to my family. They had grown up in the atmosphere of the old populist movement, of which their own parents had been very much a part. My father's family had immigrated to Nebraska from Ireland during the 1860s. The Homestead Act of 1862 opened public lands in the West to free settlement by American citizens or those who, like my grandparents, declared their intention of becoming citizens. Even in the best of times, things were never easy for long on a farm. The country was still largely rural near the end of the nineteenth century, but the cities were growing, both in number and in economic and political power. The farmers' uneasiness about the future and their increasing economic difficulties gave rise to a broad-based agrarian movement that began in the midwestern heartland and spread like wildfire throughout much of the South. My grandfather got swept up in this populist struggle. In the 1880s he ran for office and won a seat in the Nebraska State Legislature, where he served alongside William Jennings Bryan—who would go on to become the Democratic candidate for president three times.

In the years leading up to the 1896 election, Bryan was a main force in organizing farmers, calling for federal action to correct what he saw as an unequal balance of power between farmers and laborers on the one hand, and industrialists and eastern bankers on the other. My grandfather, like the majority of farmers in Nebraska, supported Bryan for president in 1896. But it was more than friendship that motivated him; it was what Bryan stood for. Running through the populists' message was a protest against exploitation and greed. The populist movement's success was limited, but it did put into words the longing for equality and justice that later found its way into the progressive movement and the New Deal. It is a language that grew out of the people and one that I, as a politician, feel comfortable with. It is part of my own family tradition and has important historical roots in our country.

Farmers weren't alone in their interest in reform. In the cities at the turn of the century there were many middle-class reformers, including suffragists and intellectuals, followers of progressive president Teddy Roosevelt and Woodrow Wilson, muckrakers, labor unionists, and social workers. They all wanted government to get rid of great disparities in income, to rescue the poor, to clean up politics, and to restore opportunities to common people. Because of their efforts, the federal government did take on a new role for itself, getting into matters that, up to then, were considered none of its business. Child labor was restricted, an income tax was levied on the wealthiest Americans, government began to regulate some industries, to help try to clean up the slums, and to make the political process somewhat more democratic. The work of these reformers laid much of the groundwork for the even more profound federal reforms under President Franklin D. Roosevelt.

I arrived in Washington steeped in my own family history and ready to continue the battle to make the government more responsive to its citizens. I agreed with Hubert Humphrey, who said: "The moral test of government is how that government treats those who are in the dawn of life, the children; those who are in the twilight of life, the elderly; and those who are in the shadows of life, the sick, the needy, and the handicapped."

A great deal had been accomplished. We had Social Security and Medicare to protect the elderly and Aid to Families with Dependent Children (AFDC) to help the poor. But the battle was not over. I wanted to focus on removing the barriers to education, employment, and health care that so many Americans faced. The inflation of the 1970s slowed our progress in knocking down those barriers, but if the 1970s seemed inhospitable, the 1980s were downright hostile. Ronald Reagan's economic and social policies broke with our country's historical commitment to ensure its citizens equality and opportunity. The president apparently felt that the rich were making too little money and the poor too much. To rectify the situation, he thought we should cut the taxes of the rich and the programs of the poor. To put it another way, the Reagan administration pruned the government that it did not like and gave a blank check to the government it did.

The administration focused on cutting government spending and taxes in order to stimulate the private sector to step in and launch a much-needed economic recovery. But these policies had another, more troublesome, purpose in mind: to shrink the size of the federal government and to eliminate its role in giving a hand-up to citizens left behind. The president said as much in his first inaugural address when he claimed that "government is not the solution to our problem, government is the problem." As Budget Director David Stockman was later to note, the Reagan proposals were nothing less than a Trojan Horse for accomplishing a severely scaled-back government.

Education, training, employment, social services, health, income security, and the administration of justice were targeted for the deepest spending cuts, and at the same time, significant increases to defense programs were demanded. The stated goal was to reduce the size and scope of the government, but the military was not considered part of "the problem." Spending cuts came from the domestic side of the budget and fully one third came from just two areas, health and income security—programs designed to meet the needs of the poor.[2] These massive spending cuts reflected a philosophy that held that welfare programs encouraged an "acceptance of indolence, promiscuity, easy abortion, casual attitudes toward marriage and divorce, and maternal indifference to child-rearing responsibilities."[3] Conservatives seemed to believe that welfare programs were largely to blame for the increasing prevalence of female-headed households.

Shortly after the administration submitted its budget to Congress, the Congressional Caucus for Women's Issues held a meeting to discuss ways to blunt its effect. With so many of our programs on the chopping block, we felt we needed to act together to be effective. We hoped to combat these excessive and punitive budget proposals because we knew that women and children would be hit the hardest by them.

The facts we were getting showed that at least one sixth of the families receiving federal assistance for dependent children would lose all or part of their benefits, including health care. The Medicaid program, which provides care to the poor and disabled, was cut; eligibility for food stamps was tightened; federal nutrition programs were to be eliminated or substantially reduced; fuel assistance programs would be cut by 25 percent; and more than nine billion dollars would be cut from commitments for housing assistance. Elementary and secondary education programs were targeted for similiar cuts, and the eligibility of college students applying for guaranteed loans would be seriously restricted. The administration cleverly packaged its cuts in health service programs, social service programs, and energy funding for low-income Americans by proposing they be consolidated into four block grants to the states. In addition they wanted to slash by at least one quarter the total amount alloted. When people complained about the results of these cuts, they would be referred to the states. The program should have been called Blame Sharing, because it gave the administration the opportunity to pass the buck to the states without providing the local governments with the money or the control needed to handle the responsibility.

Ronald Reagan's economic and social policies would mean an abrupt change of course for social policy in the United States. What poor families needed was job training, child care, and health benefits so they could become self-sufficient. What the conservatives offered was the promise of a vigorous economy that would "trickle down" and help those on the bottom rung of society. I ran into a wonderful person five years after Reagan came to office. He said he and his family had been waiting and waiting for five years for the trickle-down, but they were not even damp yet!

It was hard not to see the attack on the poor as an assault on women: nearly three out of every five persons with incomes below the poverty level were women, as were two out of every three older persons living in poverty. In fact, in 1981, households headed by females made up 11 percent of all households and 27 percent of all poverty households. The truth was that families headed by females with no spouse were three times more likely to be living in poverty than all other families.[4] Divorce, widowhood, unemployment, low pay, and lack of child support and affordable housing are some of the causes of poverty among women. These problems get a lot worse when programs like AFDC or Medicaid are cut. And when we deny aid to female heads of households we are really punishing the millions of children who depend on them. We have such a large middle class in this country partly because we have always provided access to education, job training, and community services. Without these, Americans on the economic margins of society can have little hope of ever making it out of poverty.

Fearing the impact of budget cuts on low-income families, Congress established the Select Committee on Children, Youth, and Families. I became a charter member and the chair of its Economic Security Task Force. I hoped to use the task force to help keep families from falling through the cracks in our economy. Between 1981 and 1984 we were able to limit the damage to social programs. There were decreases in AFCD, food stamps, Medicaid, and public housing, but they were significantly less than what the administration requested. We were also able to ward off efforts to eliminate the program for Women, Infants, and Children (WIC), a supplemental food program that had reduced infant mortality, decreased the number of low-birth-weight babies, and lowered future federal health care costs. The principal beneficiaries of these programs were female heads of households.

Despite our damage-control campaign, between 1982 and 1985, 325,000 families lost eligibility for aid to families with dependent children and an additional 325,000 to 350,000 had their benefits reduced; about one million people lost eligibility for food stamps; and the number of pupils in federally subsidized school lunch programs dropped by three million.

Further, the promise of "trickle-down" didn't materialize after the tax cuts, and by 1986 the number of poor families had increased by 35 percent. The Center on Budget and Policy Priorities reported, "One third of the increase in poverty among families with children since 1979 would not have occurred if government programs had as much impact today [1986] in removing families from poverty as the programs did in 1979." The impact was even more marked for families headed by women with children: "The proportion of poor female-headed families with children lifted from poverty by the programs was cut nearly in half" during the period between 1979 and 1986.[5]

Budget cuts were not the only reason for the growing number of poor. Changes in the economy, including high unemployment, inflation, and back-to-back recessions in the early 1980s, together with high divorce rates, contributed to the increasing number of poor female-headed households and the doubling rate of poor young families.

The alarming growth of the number of poor women was called the feminization of poverty. At first it was thought about as another "women's issue." But it soon became clear that much more was involved. A growing number of poor women were new to poverty. They were mothers who because of divorce had become single parents, or mid-life or older women who had never married or who had recently been widowed. Single motherhood and poverty became more intertwined. In 1960, only 25 percent of all poor families were headed by women, whereas today, 56 percent of all poor families are headed by a single woman.[6] By 1984, according to the Women's Bureau of the Department of Labor, there were 9.9 million mothers living with children under twenty-one years of age whose fathers were not in the household.[7]

One sixth of all American families were maintained by women and about one out of five children in the United States lives with a single mother. One estimate for the future is that about 42 percent of all white children and about 86 percent of all black children born in the late 1970s will live in a family headed by a single woman at some time before they reach the age of eighteen.[8]

The myth that most women on welfare were born into welfare families has also been found to be incorrect. In most states, a majority of the women on welfare first confronted poverty after a divorce or separation. A major drop in living standards for women and children is almost universal following divorce. According to one study, "Nearly half of such families enter poverty."[9] Both middle-class and poor women usually assume sole financial responsibility for their children. In 1979, only 59 percent of mothers with at least one child eligible for support were awarded support payments. The amount of most of these payments could not adequately support a child. Further, of those who were awarded child support, only 49 percent ever got the full amount and 28 percent of women got nothing.[10]

Why the sums granted by the courts so often bear so little relation to the cost of raising a child puzzles me. In 1985, the average annual payment was, as *The New York Times* put it, "a pitiful $2,500 a year."[11] It is still more amazing that the courts don't award even that small amount to almost half the families.

On a flight to Denver a couple of years ago, I met a young stewardess, a single parent, who told me that her husband wasn't keeping up with child support payments and that she wasn't getting any help from the state to force him to pay up. She told me she worried all the time, and she wanted to know if there wasn't something that could be done to make the child's father live up to his obligations. The fact is that even if the state of Colorado did manage to collect what was due her, it wasn't likely to help all that much. Colorado courts awarded paltry sums: two thirds of Colorado fathers had been ordered to pay less per month for child support than they spent for their car payments.[12]

Divorced women all across the country have been writing to me for help in collecting child support for years. Since the enforcement of the divorce laws rests with the states, and each state has a different policy, there has not been a lot we could do on a case-by-case basis except to give out information regarding existing laws and remedies. But as the problem mushroomed, it became clear that national enforcement procedures were necessary. States were clearly neglecting their responsibility to enforce child support payments, and absent parents apparently felt no obligation to pay. In fact, it seems to me that the states' inaction leads to a feeling that nonpayment is okay. If you could put down a payment on a car, move it to another state, and avoid further payments, people would demand that the federal government step in. The federal government should care as much about child support as it does about car payments!

Strengthening child support laws became a top priority for the Congressional Caucus for Women's Issues. Our first concern was to find a way to enforce the existing child support statutes and make parents pay what the court had awarded to the child. In 1975, Congress had enacted the Child Support Enforcement program, which provided matching funds to help the states locate absent parents, establish paternity, and obtain support payments. Basic responsibility remained with the states, but the federal government would fund, monitor, and evaluate state programs and provide technical assistance. From nearly nothing before 1975, collections approached about two billion dollars by 1983 and paternity determinations increased from 173,000 in 1978 to 750,000 in 1982.[13]

The quality of state programs varied dramatically: six states had collected 88 percent of the funds, while the other states and territories collected only 12 percent.[14] I was amazed that the federal government had to be dragged into this issue. If the parents didn't support their children, the federal government did. It seemed to me that the situation would make the government very interested in firing up state action.

In 1983, Rep. Barbara Kennelly, Democrat from Connecticut, introduced legislation that called on all states to establish enforcement procedures with income withholding, expedited legal processes, extended deadlines for establishing paternity, expanded systems for enforcing support orders, and improved enforcement of interstate cases. The legislation required states to establish a system for mandatory wage withholding if support payments were thirty days overdue. If someone was in arrears, the state was required to deduct the outstanding claim from income tax refunds, or to take liens against property, and to see that bonds, securities, or guarantees were posted to ensure payment by the noncustodial parent who had been lax in meeting legal obligations. The federal government provided matching funds for the states' cost of enforcement.

This bill went a long way to bringing some regularity to the enforcement process, and I worked with the other congresswomen to see that it passed. It did seem to me that waiting until child support payments became delinquent before enforcing the withholding provision was not the most efficient way. The process should be automatic for everyone; then there would be no stigma attached to it. I introduced a separate bill calling for automatic assignment of federal civil service employees' wages when child support is ordered, modified, or enforced by states. I made the argument that the government, as the largest employer in the country, ought to provide the most efficient mechanism for employees to meet their legal obligation to support their children. Setting up such a standard would establish a model program for private-sector child support enforcement. But the idea of automatic garnishment did not catch on then, even for federal employees. As a result, the month-to-month hassle of child support collection continued.

Congresswoman Kennelly's bill moved quickly through the House with considerable support from liberals and conservatives alike. The latter saw the bill as a way to make fathers live up to their parental obligations and to cut federal expenditures. The Reagan administration also joined the effort, though not until the two prominent female Republican Cabinet members, Margaret M. Heckler, then Secretary of Health and Human Services, and Elizabeth H. Dole, then Secretary of Transportation, convinced them that this was the way to go. In August 1984, the Senate and the House unanimously passed the bill.

The Child Support Enforcement Amendment was an important achievement because it made clear that the federal government had a role to play when the economic security of families and children was at stake. But at least two serious problems remained: first, the federal legislation did not standardize the process for setting award levels; and second, not all states had effective enforcement procedures. There were no national and few statewide standards for what child support should be. In most places, the amount awarded depended on the individual court. Procedures for withholding were scarce because an expensive and complex computer system was necessary to automate the process.

Collection of child support has improved considerably over the years, but according to estimates by the Department of Health and Human Services' Office on Child Support Enforcement, at least $9 billion in payments were overdue in the fiscal year of 1986, and this is a very conservative estimate. At least 40 percent of women with children are not even eligible to receive child support. Half the families due child support from an absent parent still don't get the money. Rep. Marge Roukema, a Republican from New Jersey, has introduced new legislation to get delinquent parents to pay up. Her bill calls for immediate automatic garnishment. That is the only way to ensure that defaults don't take place. If this bill passes, withholding will be automatic for *all* employees who owe child support. All court-ordered child support awards will be immediately processed for automatic withholding.

Even if a perfect child support system was in place, single mothers would face serious difficulties in supporting their families. The most problematic is wages. Although a majority of women work outside the home, they remain concentrated in low-paying jobs that often do not provide health or pension benefits or adequate sick leave, vacation, and family and medical leave. In 1981, the median earnings of women who worked full-time, year-round, was $12,001, or 59 percent of the $20,260 that men earned. Today, for the one of every five women workers who maintains a family on her own, the disparity in wages has especially serious consequences for the health and well-being of her children.[15]

Despite their lower wages, married women (with husbands

present) contribute a median of 26.7 percent of family income. In families with less than $10,000 annual income, the woman's contribution is 69 percent; it is 46.6 percent if family income is between $15,000 and $19,000. Minority women make even larger economic contributions to family income.[16] Women's earnings have made the critical difference for families in maintaining or improving their standards of living in the 1970s and 1980s, *even though* their earnings are lower than men's.

One of the main reasons for the pay gap is that women are "sexagrated." Almost half of all employed women work in occupations that are at least 80 percent female. Four fifths of all women work in only 25 occupations out of the 420 total listed by the U.S. Department of Labor. If a profession is made up mostly of women, it is, by definition, low-paying. Women make up 99.1 percent of the nation's secretaries, 97.8 of the registered nurses, 84.5 percent of elementary school teachers, 82 percent of librarians, 98.3 percent of cleaning and household service workers, and 86.3 percent of clerks.[17] Our society runs on these jobs, but because women do them—and the traditional assumption has been that women do not need to earn as much as men because someone else helps support them—all of these occupations, like others in which women predominate, are poorly paid. A study by Heidi Hartman and Barbara Reskin found that "each additional percentage point female in an occupation was associated with $42 less in median annual incomes."[18]

It is hard for women to break out of female-dominated occupations. I faced some of these problems getting my first job. In 1964, when I was finishing my law degree at Harvard, I went into the placement office to begin looking for a job. The placement officer told me he thought it best that I not look for work with a law firm. He said, "No firm will hire a young married woman like you because they know you will be having children soon and they see it as a waste of time." He told me that firms would interview me if I insisted, but that I would never be hired. I did have several interviews with law firms—and was invariably asked if I could type! Since I wanted to practice law, I kept on looking and soon accepted the offer of a job in the federal government. Obviously my choices were more limited than those of the male graduates of Harvard. No one ever told Jim, after the same three grueling years of study, that since he was sure to be a father sometime in the future, he should think about another kind of work!

Breaking patterns of occupational segregation and pay discrimination has not been easy. In 1982, Rep. Geraldine Ferraro, Rep. Mary Rose Oakar, and I, as chairwomen of the subcommittees on Human Resources, Compensation and Employee Benefits, and Civil Service respectively, held a series of joint hearings on the problem of occupational segregation and its solutions in pay equity, affirmative action programs, and enforcement of existing federal antidiscrimination laws.

We were not the first to attack this problem. There had been several court decisions ordering states to study and remedy pay inequity. However, the federal government, the largest single employer, had not addressed the problem and continued to set wages according to a rating system established in 1923. Nobody in the intervening sixty-five years had tried to find out whether the wages and classifications accurately reflected the modern work force. During the hearings on pay equity, I presented testimony that showed that 62 percent of women in the federal system work in occupations that are overwhelmingly female. Few women find their way into nontraditional jobs in the federal government. Women in the white-collar sector are ghettoized in a few professions. Men work at different jobs; ergo, men earn more. That is the way the system operates in federal employment as well as in the private sector. (It should be noted that the same pay discrepancies occurred in other countries as the workplace changed and women entered the work force, but those countries have been much quicker to close the gap than we have.) As a result of the hearings, Representative Oakar introduced the first pay equity bill as part of the Economic Equity Act. It passed the House by a vote of 413 to 6, but it went nowhere in the Republican-controlled Senate. Conservatives in the administration and at the Commission on Civil Rights attacked the bill. The late Clarence Pendleton, then head of the commission, called the concept of pay equity or comparable worth "the looniest idea since looney tunes itself."

The conservative philosophy was that the free market should be the final arbiter of wages. But what they failed to recognize or chose to ignore was that employers have been setting wage levels by comparing various job components for decades. The problem is that they have refused to look at the component of sex descrimination. Since the Senate did not act on the bill, it died.

In the next term, the bill passed the House again, this time by a much narrower margin because the conservatives were on the warpath. Again, the Senate took no action. I find it incredible that Congress is unwilling even to call for a study of the current pay structure—devised in 1923—to determine if it contains sex discrimination. These pay issues have a direct effect on our economic security because of the growing number of women who head our families. The government collects taxes equally from women and men, but it fails to recognize pay discrimination and how it lowers America's standard of living and makes it much harder for families to improve their lives.

Pay equity, the state of the economy, inflation, unemployment, access to education, changes in employment patterns, decent wages, and federal tax policies are all factors that help determine the economic well-being of families. As a lawmaker, I believe it is my job to keep one eye on the larger picture: the major economic forces that are in play and the ways that federal policies can influence them. One disturbing trend emerging over the last decade is a growing inequality in the distribution of family income. According to the Joint Economic Committee, the share of national income going to the richest 20 percent of the population was larger in the 1980s than at any other time in the postwar period. At the same time, the share going to the poorest 40 percent fell to its lowest point.[19]

Not everyone agrees on why this has occurred, or what can or should be done about it. But the effects of this disparity are severe on young families and families headed by single women. The real incomes of families headed by people under twenty-five, and families with children and no full-time, full-year workers, were between 10 and 20 percent lower in 1986 than the incomes of their counterparts sixteen years earlier. Two fifths of all young families with children had incomes at or below the poverty level in 1986. Earnings for low-income single women with children followed a similar pattern: there was an overall drop of 13 percent between 1970 and 1986. This has meant that many single mothers have had less than half the income needed to live even at the poverty level with their children.[20]

People at the lowest income levels are not the only ones slipping behind. The worker who lost his $35,000-a-year job because the company moved its plant overseas now may earn only $22,000. His wife must work to fill the gap. Now, rising costs and the need for child care mean that families have less money and less opportunity to better themselves.

In July 1987, the Select Committee on Children, Youth, and Families took a look at the family's long-term prospects for economic security. Is it possible for families to provide the basic necessities of life: housing, education, health care, and care for the elderly? We knew that Americans had been adjusting to the new economic realities by delaying marriage and childbirth, by having fewer children, by sending more family members into the work force, and by going into debt at unprecedented rates.[21] But what promise did the future hold for them, despite such measures?

The rising cost of basic family obligations, combined with declining family income, has meant that the average family is working harder just to stand still. That certainly is true when young people want to buy a home. One young couple told me that even with husband and wife working full-time, they hadn't been able to put together enough money to buy a house. They had both been working for six or seven years, but with the high mortgage rates and the ever-escalating cost of property, they despaired of finding anything they could afford.

Lately, the dream of owning your own home is becoming less and less attainable. In 1985, the Joint Economic Committee found that a thirty-year-old man in 1973 would need 21 percent of his pay for carrying charges for a median-priced home. By 1984, a typical thirty-year-old man with the same kind of home would have had to devote 44 percent of his gross monthly income to carrying charges. It is not surprising, then, that home ownership rates for young households fell from 23.4 percent in 1973 to 19.4 percent in 1983. Of those young couples fortunate enough to buy a house, almost one third received financial assistance from their relatives; only 10 percent relied on a relative's help in 1978.

Congress made a historic commitment to the American family almost forty years ago when it passed the Housing Act of 1949. The Housing Act states that it is the policy of the United States that every American family have "a decent home . . . in a suitable environment." In the following years, with government help, a great deal of housing was constructed. Then, during the Reagan years, this promise was broken. As one witness noted at the Select Committee hearing, "For the first time [since 1949], the steady march toward home ownership has come to a halt." Ownership rates have declined by 16 percent for young families (householders under twenty-five years of age) between 1980 and 1985 alone.

People wanting to buy homes are not the only ones having trouble. The fall in home ownership has increased competition for fewer and fewer rental units, and rents have skyrocketed. The government's commitment for housing units fell from 300,000 units per year in the 1970s, to about 100,000 per year in the 1980s. In the same period the number of families that are ill-housed, living in crowded substandard units or housing costing more than 30 percent of their income, increased to a record twelve to fourteen million families. For the first time in recent history, the United States has no family housing policy to speak of. The growing numbers of homeless families are a direct result of the federal government's abandoning its commitment.

A similar picture emerges in education. Politicians love to evoke the refrain that an investment in education for our children is an investment in the future of the country. No politician ever has gotten elected running against education, but during the last decade, the conservatives sought to balance the federal budget by cutting appropriations to schools at every educational level. Overall federal spending for education decreased about 14.3 percent between 1981 and 1985. Had Congress acceded to the total administration budget requests for the period, spending for education would have fallen 36 percent after inflation. A disproportionate share of the cuts, roughly 40 percent, came out of the federal contribution to elementary and secondary education.[22] Everyone—students, teachers, local communities, and the nation as a whole—pays a high price for this policy.

Public education has been the bedrock of the American tradition for over two hundred years. Thomas Jefferson requested that he be remembered on his tombstone not as the third president of the United States but as "the author of the Declaration of American Independence, of the Statute of Virginia for Religious Freedom, and Father of the University of Virginia." But the government's policies in recent years have been a travesty of this ideal. Federal support for public education has been eroded because of idealogical showmanship. Teachers have been made the scapegoats for falling test scores. We've heard more about school prayer than about raising teachers' salaries. As Albert Einstein once commented, "Any society that pays master plumbers more than master teachers will soon have neither." Education is expensive but ignorance is national suicide.

We cannot afford the current dropout rate of one out of seven students nationwide, with much worse figures in some of our cities. Our young people will need more education, not less, to compete in the highly competitive global economy in which they will live. The nature of our economy has changed enormously and the rapid change continues. There will be fewer manufacturing jobs, and many of the sons and daughters of steelworkers and auto workers will not be able to follow in their parents' footsteps into well-paid jobs. In today's market, far more education, training, and special skills are required than were necessary for the jobs that are disappearing.

Workers with insufficient education have already taken a beating in the 1970s. Among thirty-year-old couples who have a high school education or less, the pay of the typical husband dropped from $20,970 in 1973 to $17,500 in 1986 in dollars adjusted for inflation.[23] Yet a college education is becoming harder and harder for families to afford. Since 1980, there are very few American families whose income is rising as fast as the cost of college. College costs have outstripped both family income and per capita income over the last ten years. To make the situation worse, at the same time that so many families were being priced out of college, the Department of Education was seeking to reverse the historical federal commitment to increasing access to education. In 1862 a national land-grant college system was established. After World War II, we saw the G.I. Bill lead to a tremendous increase in the percentage of Americans with college degrees. In more recent years, federally supported student loans and grants helped people who would not otherwise be able to receive a college education.

A terrible reversal has taken place. Today, students are being asked to pay more tuition because federal student aid and state appropriations have not kept pace with inflation. Student grant programs have been all but eliminated. Many would-be students are priced out of the education they deserve.

It is not that they are unwilling to help themselves—close to 90 percent of part-time students work and close to 40 percent of full-time students work. There is nothing wrong with working your way through school—many of us did that. The money I earned covered almost all my costs. But today that is impossible.

Tuition has escalated way beyond the wage-earning capacity of students. Even if they work all summer for the coming school year and work part-time during the year, they still cannot keep up. Making the situation worse is that many of the student work programs that were available during the academic year have been seriously eroded. The result of rising costs and falling economic opportunities is that students, even though they are working, are forced to take out loans to finance their education. We really don't know the effects of such indebtedness. At the present time students may borrow upwards of $25,000 to finance four years of college—and if they go on to graduate or professional school, they may owe twice that amount. This huge debt may limit their future decisions with respect to jobs, career, family plans, and other significant financial undertakings.

My own parents and grandparents went to college, and my family believed everyone had a right to such education but also a responsibility to work for it. My mom taught us to work diligently and purposefully, but as a public school teacher she believed that going to college should be a right of citizenship. But she did not mean it should be a handout. My own experience at the University of Minnesota taught me firsthand about working for what you got. Minnesota was a "streetcar college"—the majority of students lived at home and commuted to class, and many worked at part-time jobs. As I often say in commencement speeches, "They sacrificed things for wings," and they went on to achieve great things for themselves. But in the early 1960s, the economy seemed to promise much more than it does now, and very few students graduated in debt.

I think our national government has an obligation to invest in strong, vibrant educational programs and to provide the opportunities for young people and adults to go to college. The government does not have to pay for it all, but a college diploma should not be for the rich only. There should be no debate about providing equal opportunities for education. It is a question of redefining our national strength: it is the level of intellectual and creative achievement we offer all our young people, rather than the number of nuclear missiles we have somewhere in a stockpile.

The escalating cost and inaccessibility of health care is another major family crisis. Thirty-seven million nonelderly Americans—one out of every six—have no health insurance. This represents a 15 percent increase since 1982 alone. In 1985, two thirds of the uninsured lived in families with children. Today, about one in five children has no health insurance coverage of any kind. Children living with single parents fare much worse.[24]

Why is this? One of the main reasons is that the costs of health care insurance have been increasing at an average annual rate of 9 percent, much faster than the average family income has increased. Between 1980 and 1985 health care costs rose 52 percent. It is hard to see an end in sight.

When my family gets together I always tease my parents that if they had had to pay what it costs to have a baby today, they might have thought twice about bringing my brother and me into the world. On August 9, 1940, St. Vincent's hospital in Portland, Oregon, billed my parents a total of $53.35 for my birth. The delivery room cost $12.00 and the ten-day stay cost $30.00. Baby care cost $5.00 and the rest was for medicine and lab tests. Even at that price, my parents paid the bill in two installments. Today, the average delivery costs about $3,000 for a three-day stay. Each additional day costs approximately $1,800. Nearly fifteen million American women of childbearing age have no private or government health insurance that covers maternity. Each year more than half a million women give birth without any health insurance protection.[25] And many of those who do have health care coverage must pay part of the insured costs.

Changes in the job market have contributed to the declining numbers of Americans receiving health care. Many people have moved into the service sector, where wages are typically low and benefits, such as health insurance, are nonexistent. Contrary to popular myth over 80 percent of uninsured Americans are either workers or nonworking spouses or dependents of workers.[26] Most private insurance coverage in the United States is provided by employer plans, but employers are not compelled to provide such insurance, and as premiums rise, fewer employers are extending coverage to their work force. In a tight economy they find it hard to compete against companies that do not provide health benefits.

Those who say that this situation is not serious because people can buy their own health policy are totally out of touch with reality. The cost of a health care policy for an individual is extremely high. Group policies offer the only possibility for most families to afford coverage.

Access to care has also declined because of cuts in Medicaid, the federal and state health program for the poor. Recent years have brought tighter eligibility requirements and thereby reduced the number of Medicaid participants. State income limits for would-be recipients have failed to keep pace with inflation. As a result, the percentage of low-income Americans under Medicaid coverage dropped from 63 percent in 1965 to 50 percent in 1985.[27]

This country does not have to provide and pay for health care for everyone, but it certainly should make sure it is available to everyone. We are not meeting this responsibility at the present time, especially not to our families. Access to health care should be the joint responsibility of government and of the business community. One suggestion—mandating that all employers offer health insurance to all their employees—is a step in the right direction. If the costs of health care were shared over a greater number of employers, this might have the benefit of lowering costs for everyone. It also might motivate employers to use their clout to help keep health care costs from escalating, rather than simply to drop coverage when the price gets too high. The federal government should do its part by making sure that Medicaid covers all poor families and also helps those who are working their way up out of poverty but are not yet eligible for health insurance under an employer-sponsored plan.

Long-term care is, at present, not covered either by the government or by most of the business community. Such costs are largely borne by the elderly and their families. Expansion of the Medicare system in 1988 through the Catastrophic Health Care Insurance Act closed many holes in health care coverage for acute illness but left unresolved the problem of care for the chronically ill. The problems and costs of home care and nursing-home care fall heavily on family members, often depleting their resources and savings and leaving them emotionally and economically drained. Many older people who have had to put a spouse in a nursing home can afford institutional care for only a short time. Then, because Medicare does not pay for long-term health care, they must use up all their assets before they can qualify for help. Husbands and wives who saved for retirement find that the economics of failing health rob them of the rewards of a lifetime of work.

Rep. Olympia Snowe, Republican from Maine and cochair of the Congressional Caucus for Women's Issues, introduced a bill as part of the Economic Equity Act in 1987 to ensure that the at-home spouses of institutionalized persons will not be left impoverished. Institutional care in a nursing home averages about $22,000 a year, a cost few families can absorb for long. Congresswoman Snowe's bill proposed to raise the limit on resources the at-home spouses could retain as well as the monthly income they could receive. The bill's provisions passed as part of the Catastrophic Health Care package at the end of the Hundredth Congress. Instead of spending down to all but $2,800 in assets, the at-home spouse will now be able to retain between $12,000 and $60,000 in resources. In addition, the limit on income level will rise significantly.

We are an aging society and we must strengthen our commitment to our senior citizens. There is a lot of talk today about intergenerational equity, about the need to direct resources away from the elderly and to the children. I think, for all the concerns our children face, we should not pit one group against another. With declining federal revenues and the enormous budget deficit, the fight over resources will intensify unless we provide leadership in showing how everyone will benefit if we care for our older citizens. It is, again, a question of defining how we want to spend our money.

It seems to me we must put the family first, not any one part of it but young and old alike, children, teenagers, young adults, parents, and grandparents. The important thing is to keep in mind the interrelationship and interdependence of families. Increasingly families with growing children are also having to take care of aging parents. To help them at one end to cope with the demands of education makes sense; not to help them at the other end with long-term care for the elderly hurts everyone. Government is built upon the small foundation blocks called families. If those blocks crumble, government crumbles.

The tax code is an important tool in creating economic opportunities for families. Since 1913, when the income tax was first introduced, tax rates have been based on the ability to pay: the more income you receive above the basic cost of living, the more you pay. Even after 1948, when more Americans began paying taxes, the idea was that you ought to pay very little tax until your income was well past the median. For that reason, more than three quarters of median-level family income was exempt from taxes through combined personal and standard deductions.[28]

By 1983, the situation had almost completely reversed itself. Families began paying taxes not when they reached the median income but when their incomes were one third the median. Even people with incomes below the poverty level were taxed. One explanation of what happened is that inflation had badly eroded the value of the personal exemption. Eugene Steurle, a Treasury Department economist, found that the $600 personal exemption in 1948 offset an average of 42 percent of per capita income. If that same 42 percent had been applied to 1984 income, you would have received a personal exemption of $5,600. In fact, our personal deduction had risen only to $1,000.

Another important shift in the tax burden is that families with children pay relatively more than families without dependents. The average tax rate for a single person or for couples with no dependents has remained the same since 1960, but for a couple with two children it was 43 percent and for couples with four dependents it rose 223 percent.

A 1981 tax cut reduced rates across the board, but because it did not index the personal exemption, the standard deduction, or the earned income tax credit, it accelerated tax penalties against families. The cuts imposed tax increases on lower-income people and gave substantial reductions to those of upper income. The federal tax burden on families at or below the poverty line increased dramatically: between 1980 and 1984 a family of four at the poverty level had its taxes increased from $462 to $1,079. Many families who were below the poverty line in 1980 and did not pay income taxes now had to pay them. The effect of the trickle-down philosophy was that those at the top had their tax burden lessened and those at the bottom have as yet to feel any economic benefit.

Nor was this the end of it. Between 1984 and 1986, Washington became consumed by "tax simplification." Tax reform plans emerged from every quarter: Sen. Bill Bradley, the Treasury Department, Rep. Robert Kasten and Rep. Jack Kemp, and several others floated plans for overhauling the system. The efforts rose and fell a dozen times before the momentum finally took hold. Although the majority of the plans called for tax fairness, I became increasingly concerned about how families were going to do under these schemes. Whose "fairness" were they talking about? The halls of Congress were lined with tax lobbyists, noted as much for their stylish attire as for the special business interests they represented. I wasn't convinced that the lobbyists stalking

"Gucci gulch" cared much about how the average family would manage when the bill finally took shape.

To make sure any future tax program would treat families as if they mattered, I called for a hearing in the Select Committee on Children, Youth, and Families. We found that by 1985, the loopholes, shelters, depletion allowances, and accelerated cost-recovery systems were all geared to interests other than families. Taxwise, you would do better raising animals than children. You can, even after the tax reform package of 1986, deduct all costs associated with raising greyhounds or horses. If you are raising children, no matter what the real expenses are, you get a $2,000-a-year exemption, an impossibly low sum that bears no relation to the actual costs of raising a child. These costs are enormous. The United States Department of Agriculture estimated that in 1984 it cost $80,000 to raise a child from birth to age eighteen, or about $4,555 a year, and that figure is before college!

Families receive fewer tax breaks than businesses do. In 1950, 40 percent of all income tax was paid by business, but by 1985, that figure had dropped to 20 percent. In the 1950s and 1960s, corporate taxes contributed 25 percent of all federal tax revenues: by 1980 corporate taxes contributed 12 percent. By 1983, after the tax changes, corporate taxes provided only 6.2 percent of federal tax revenues. The loss in income was enormous. In 1983, corporations received $1.60 in loopholes for every $1.00 paid in corporate taxes. Obviously, something had to be done to make up the difference. What was done by the Reagan administration was to shift the tax burdens from corporations to middle-class families.

To help redress these wrongs I introduced a bill in 1984 to make the personal exemption $2,600 for each dependent, the actual value of the then-current exemption if it were made consistent with the rise in the consumer price index. Even so, $2,600 did not come close to the $5,600 the deduction would actually be worth if it had been indexed to income growth.

The personal exemption is one of the few ways the tax code can be turned toward helping American families. The 1986 Tax

Reform Act did, in fact, double the amount of the personal deduction to $2,000. It also raised the zero bracket amount to $5,000 for
married couples, $4,400 for single heads of households, and $3,000
for single taxpayers. The positive results of these changes are
important: approximately six million families are exempt from
paying any federal income tax and an additional five million
families with low income receive significant tax reduction. The
bill also narrowed the gap between tax treatment of single heads
of households and that of married couples. A single parent with
three children and earnings at the poverty line would find that
the combined federal income and payroll taxes were reduced by
over $1,200, from $1,452 to $245—a cut of 83 percent.

Unfortunately, that was the end of the good news about the tax
act. The 1986 Tax Reform Act neither simplified the tax system
nor restored equity to the majority of American families. By
cutting the top rate almost in half and by reducing the number
of brackets from fifteen to two, the measure virtually wiped out
the concept of a progressive federal tax system. To put it another
way, families making $30,000 a year pay the same percentage as
families making one million dollars a year.

The measure also meant a tax increase for more than three
million people, 77 percent of whom have incomes below $50,000.
One observer called the new law "a gift to the rich unmatched
since Calvin Coolidge pushed through a 24 percent top rate for
1929."[29] The top rate extends far down into the middle class, so
that, for instance, a science researcher making $22,000 a year and
Lee Iacocca, who makes quite a bit more, pay the same 28 percent
marginal tax rate on income over $17,850.

What the law did was to continue the shift of the tax burden
from upper-income to middle-income individuals, especially the
middle-income group of those whose life-style the Reagan administration did not approve: two-earner couples. Tax reform
brought back the marriage penalty tax we had spent so many
years trying to get rid of. Under the new measure, couples with
one earner and a wife at home receive an income-splitting bonus

from joint filing, whereas two-earner couples will pay more taxes. In other words, well-off men, whose wives have little or no earnings, save taxes, and husbands and wives who both work pay a "penalty" in the form of higher taxes. About 40 percent of families will pay a "marriage penalty tax" averaging $1,100. The people who incur the worst marriage penalty are husbands and wives who earn about the same amount—especially low-income couples with children.[30]

The repeal of the deduction for sales taxes and for consumer interest payments and the sharp limits on deductions for medical expenses and work-related costs also hurt average Americans. Yet, along with cutting into these family deductions, the bill retained deductions for mortgages on second homes and business lunches!

Worst of all, the bill helped put the cost of a college education beyond the reach of many citizens. The interest cost on student loans no longer can be deducted, though students are becoming increasingly dependent on borrowing money to go to college and graduate school. Because of this loss, many families will not be able to afford the high monthly expense of paying back interest. Scholarships and fellowships not used for tuition or books are now taxed, effectively reducing even further already paltry stipends. Parents are finding it harder to save money for their children's college education because of sharp new limits on how much can be saved at the child's lower tax rate.

These measures work against helping families afford the American dream. The bill was designed to be revenue neutral, but along the way it shifted the tax burden so that it became "family negative." Worse, such a policy, in the face of record federal deficits, did nothing to get the country on the right track.

The country faces a difficult challenge: to bring our runaway deficit under control and to restore our commitment to America as a land of opportunity. Tax reform was a step backwards. As a fiscal conservative, I do not think that simply spending more will solve the dilemma. We need to put families at the center stage of our national interest by changing the direction of our national policy through real tax fairness: tax breaks for dependent care, for child care, and for health care.

We must give higher preference to the expenses involved in raising a family than to those for raising racehorses, for two-martini lunches, or for beach homes. We must encourage access to affordable health care and housing; we must reestablish a broad commitment to education and provide help so that all qualified people can go to college, no matter what their income level. We must also expand our commitment to the elderly and the families that care for them.

Many people shy away from questions of government economic policy, thinking that they are too complex for the average person. But if we do not monitor how the government manages its money—how it raises it as well as how it spends it—our family budgets will suffer and we, as private citizens, will have to struggle harder to stay afloat.

8

Family Problems—
Family Secrets

WITHOUT a doubt, one of the most difficult challenges of my congressional career has been to address the previously taboo problems of child abuse, domestic violence, alcoholism, and drug abuse. These complex, emotionally sensitive issues have a profound impact on family life. Their effects can reverberate for generations.

Over the years, various family problems have literally been brought home to me. Though nobody planned it, our house has become a safe haven for several of Scott's and Jamie's friends when they are having problems with their families. Jamie has said her friends like taking refuge with us because they see us as a "normal family." At first I was puzzled by that comment because on the surface we don't seem that normal to me. After all, Mom is a congresswoman, we travel a lot, and we all have very independent life-styles. What Jamie meant, I suspect, was that we are not a family at war. We have our cross words. We raise our voices. But we never give up on each other. Not so far and not ever, I'm determined.

Sometimes kids have called or shown up at three in the morning and asked if they could spend the night at our house to escape fighting parents. Once I even signed one of our young friends out of a hospital emergency room because the father was too drunk to do it. It has been quite a learning experience for me, since my own childhood was fairly protected emotionally. That doesn't mean we lived a dull life. As I've mentioned before, we were a flying family. My dad loves to joke that Mike and I were born and raised in an airplane. Some people called me a tomboy because I was adventurous and pretty fearless. My brother once described me as "the sort of child that when you threw a spider at her, she'd pick it up and throw it right back."

I loved being around people—as far as I was concerned, the more the merrier. Not one to cling to my father or hide behind my mother's skirt, I would strike up a conversation with anyone who would listen and then talk a blue streak—a quality that resulted in a harrowing experience for my mother when I was three years old and we were living in Kansas City. I don't remember a thing about the incident, but my mother says that while she was talking to a neighbor, I was out in front of the house. A man came by, began to talk to me, and offered me a toy. Luckily another neighbor saw me walking away with the stranger, realized something was wrong, and ran after us—at which time the kidnapper dropped my hand and tore down the road, outrunning my rescuers.

There was, however, one thing about my childhood that was different from other people's—my eye problems. I woke up one morning when I was very young, and suddenly my eyes were crossed. The diagnosis was amblyopia, a condition where a "lazy" eye weakens from lack of use. I was fitted for corrective glasses at the age of one and half. Today, when I am in grocery stores and see eighteen-month-old babies in strollers, I can't believe I had to wear glasses at that age. My poor parents finally had to strap them to my head because I kept batting them off. For years, my mother would have to help me with daily eye exercises and I came to dread them as much as some of my other friends dreaded their piano lessons. In my early school years I had to wear an eyepatch, alternating the eye to be covered.

My depth perception was so poor that it limited the kinds of activities I could participate in, especially athletics. With a patch over my eye, I wasn't exactly a number-one draft choice for the kickball team. And a young girl with an eyepatch is going to get teased. Kids would come up to me, no matter what city we were living in, and tell me I looked like a pirate. And they would ask questions like "Do you have a glass eye?" or "What are you hiding behind the patch?" (Little did I know then that being peppered with personal questions would be good preparation for my career in politics.) At first, these inquiries startled me because, having always assumed I was normal, I couldn't understand why kids were reacting to me as if I were some kind of freak. Fighting their attitude toward me became just as much a challenge as strengthening my eyes. I was unprepared for all the barbs, and they were keenly felt, but I compensated for them by concentrating more on my schoolwork and by developing a sense of humor. Whenever I was teased, I always smiled and dished it back with humor. As my father used to remind me, "Never frown at your enemies. Smile—it scares the hell out of them."

There was some concern as to whether I'd have my full eyesight as an adult, but, luckily, I do have great two-dimensional vision. The experience with my eyes, however, helped me to understand more clearly the sense of isolation felt by those whose problems—physical and emotional—are much more serious than mine. In hearings and in letters from the physically impaired and others, I have been told stories of terrifying fear, lost hope, shattered dreams, and pervasive loneliness: a woman is afraid her abusive ex-husband will return to hurt her and her kids; a teenager feels so alienated from her alcoholic parents that she contemplates suicide; parents who, abused themselves as children, desperately want help so that they will not harm their own sons and daughters. Violence, neglect, alcoholism, and drug abuse poison a family's environment and imperil its ability to function. The secrecy that often shrouds these problems can further damage the home environment and can seal the family off from possible solutions.

Two of the problems that have come to the forefront since I've been in Congress are child abuse and domestic violence. When I first campaigned for Congress, I said I wanted to be a voice for the powerless and the vulnerable members of our society. Soon after I was elected, I had the opportunity to live up to those words. Three months after I was sworn in as a congresswoman, Sen. Walter Mondale, chairman of the Senate Committee on Children and a true champion of children's issues, called and asked if I would consider sponsoring as my first legislation a bill on the disturbing problem of child abuse.

Denver is the home of the National Training Center for Child Abuse and Neglect, a widely acclaimed facility that has done pioneering work in the field. I knew about its multidisciplinary, team-oriented system of counseling, which uses social workers, psychiatrists, psychologists, and lay therapists. It has been very successful in treating abusive parents and deterring them from further abuse. Because I was familiar with the problem and cared about it a great deal, I agreed to become the House sponsor of the legislation and immediately began to do my homework.

Child abuse is not a new problem. Since colonial days, there have been laws making the cruel treatment of children a crime. But the concept that people or communities have a moral obligation to intervene to protect a child who is being physically or emotionally hurt did not emerge until early in the twentieth century with the creation of child protection agencies. However, the idea that parents can beat, burn, or physically harm a child is so repulsive that many people were reluctant to acknowledge it, much less to intercede. The problem generally remained hidden, until the early 1960s, when the United States Children's Bureau drafted a model law that required physicians to take the initiative and report instances where children had been physically abused.[1]

Within five years, all fifty states had passed child abuse reporting requirements. Yet there were tremendous gaps in the states' policies. In some states people refrained from reporting incidents because whistle-blowers were not provided with immunity from lawsuits. In many states, child protection agencies did not use standardized reporting procedures and did not have the necessary resources to conduct their investigations. Even if cases could be substantiated, there were very few places to which the parents or the child could be referred for counseling and treatment.

In an effort to ameliorate this situation Senator Mondale and I introduced the Child Abuse and Protection Act. The bill funded local demonstration and counseling programs on child abuse and tied that funding to a state's ability to meet specific reporting and treatment requirements. It also established a national center on child abuse in the federal government to spark and coordinate research and training on the problem.

The legislation was not unanimously embraced when it was first introduced. The Nixon administration, in the midst of a bitter and vigorous debate with Congress over the regulation and funding of social service programs, opposed the bill at first and even threatened to veto it. Other conservative opponents of child abuse legislation tried to direct the debate away from the welfare of the child and toward the "sanctity of the traditional American family." Conservatives argued that government has no business meddling in family affairs, that such meddling smacks of the Big Brother government George Orwell described in his book *1984*. Amid groans that liberal do-gooders were trying to usurp the American tradition of the family as a self-reliant institution, conservatives claimed that my bill was really an effort to erode the time-honored assumption that "a man's home is his castle." As I lobbied my colleagues on the bill, I heard some interesting responses. One older member told me, "Families can take care of their own problems." Another told me that one person's discipline was another person's abuse. Other legislators really did not seem to want to know that such things as child abuse go on.

The consequences of denying the problem can be tragic. I saw this when my brother, Mike, took up a custody case a few years before my election. A divorced woman had come to him because she felt that her ex-husband had been abusing their daughter during his visitation days. To find out whether she had any reason to worry, Mike went to the father's apartment building and asked neighbors if they had noticed anything unusual. No one had seen or heard anything suspicious. A couple of weeks later the child was killed, beaten to death by her father. The same neighbors who earlier had told Mike that they saw nothing were now saying that they "had always suspected child abuse." Some even mentioned seeing bruises on the little girl. This tragic loss of life might have been prevented if they had reported their suspicions. The story made a vivid impression on me and I told it to my colleagues as I lobbied them to pass legislation that might prevent such tragedies.

The House Education and Labor Subcommittee on Select Education held four hearings on my bill, and Senator Mondale's Senate Committee on Children held a special hearing in Denver. Although I wasn't a member of these committees, I attended all of the hearings. Because this was my first bill, I was anxious to learn all I could about the subject. Social workers, physicians, lawyers, and psychiatrists testified that child abuse was a complex problem. Dr. Henry Kempe, who established the Denver program and was then chairman of the University of Colorado Medical Center, had conducted ground-breaking research on the battered-child syndrome in the early 1960s and had been instrumental in fashioning an earlier model law on reporting requirements. At the Denver hearings, Dr. Kempe pointed out that, more often than not, child-abusing parents were themselves victims of abuse during their own childhood. He also told the committee that a parent may become abusive because the child reminds him of his own failure. As Dr. Kempe said, "The scapegoated child syndrome points to the need to find a civilized way to deal with parental failure."[2]

Nobody wants to be an abusing parent, but inordinate stress can overwhelm some parents and push them to the point of hurting their children. Studies have documented that when unemployment is higher, so is the incidence of child abuse. As one abusive parent wrote me, "Getting laid off from my job just proved to me that I was a loser." The C. Henry Kempe National Center for the Prevention and Treatment of Child Abuse and Neglect has been tracking the number of reported abuse cases in Colorado since 1969 and has found that physical abuse cases consistently rise and fall with the Colorado unemployment rate. The House Select Committee on Children, Youth, and Families found, in a 1987 survey of governors, that 60 percent of the states ranked poor economic conditions for families as an important reason for the rise in the number of reports of abuse and neglect.[3]

While economic stress can exacerbate abuse of all kinds, each case has its own set of contributing factors. Child abuse cuts across class lines but is more likely to occur in poor families, and, as noted, it is a behavior passed on from generation to generation. And in many families where there is child abuse, there is also spouse abuse and alcohol and drug abuse. While much abuse is committed by people who are emotionally disturbed, many abusive parents do not have chronic emotional problems but are under tremendous life pressure and take their problems out on their kids. In fact, many cases of child abuse can be prevented and treated with the aid of skilled and compassionate help. Because my legislation was targeted to provide such services to families in crisis, I came to think of it as a bill of hope and new beginnings for families, enabling them to break from their past.

Eventually, as the hearings progressed and the press called attention to the problem, child abuse became an issue no one could ignore any longer. Even the Nixon administration changed its tune and supported us. In 1973 the Child Abuse and Protection Act passed overwhelmingly.

Since the bill's passage, reports of neglect, physical abuse, sexual abuse, and emotional abuse have increased by a staggering 212 percent. In 1986, there were over two million reports of child maltreatment.[4] This increase does not necessarily mean that more parents are abusing their children; it probably indicates that more teachers, doctors, social workers, neighbors, and family members are coming forward when they suspect a child is being harmed. Two key trends appear to have spurred this increase. First, states have passed laws expanding the list of professions whose practitioners are required to report suspected cases of abuse. In California, for example, a doctor was found guilty of involuntary manslaughter for failing to report bruises and other injuries he had observed on a little girl who was later beaten to death.[5] Second, many states have broadened their definition of child abuse to include, in addition to physical harm, such mistreatment as sexual abuse, neglect, emotional abuse, medical neglect, educational neglect, and abandonment. But many people find the meaning of these terms vague and confusing. It is not unusual for teachers, when they observe children in school dressed improperly or apparently malnourished, to confuse these signs of poverty with evidence of neglect.

In spite of the increase in the number of reports, many cases of child abuse remain hidden. It has been estimated that for every case that is brought to the attention of the authorities, three are not. Conversely, about 40 percent of the reports filed with authorities are unsubstantiated, either because there is not enough information to make a determination or because the accusation is false.[6] In some states the percentage of these cases is higher; in New York, for example, 75 percent of the reports of abuse are not confirmed.[7]

Increased public awareness has had a direct effect on the growing number of child abuse reports. In the case of sexual abuse, public awareness has grown so rapidly in part because many tragic cases have been sensationalized in the press. Sexual abuse of children is a serious problem and its frequency rate seems to have skyrocketed, but the cases that attract the press tend to be the extremes that distort the problem, exaggerate people's fears, and create an atmosphere of hysteria. According to the press, sexual abuse is the new social epidemic, but in fact less than 15 percent of all child abuse cases are sexual[8].

I got a good firsthand look at public hysteria-in-the-making in

1983, when, as a member of the House Judiciary Subcommittee on Civil and Constitutional Rights, I found myself in the middle of the missing-children debate. John Walsh is a man whose son Adam had been abducted from a Florida shopping mall and was later found brutally murdered. Mr. Walsh began a movement to help parents look for children who had been kidnapped by strangers. The movement was fueled by a TV docudrama, followed by pictures of missing children, and a toll-free number to call with information on their whereabouts. The presentation was so dramatic and compelling that hundreds of communities joined in helping to look for these children. I felt deep sympathy for parents like John Walsh, but much of the testimony presented before the subcommittee made me skeptical that the problem was as widespread an epidemic as was claimed.

I hope I am never insensitive to terrible problems like kidnapping, but the fact is that I had misgivings about an overreaction. I was worried about scaring little children and their parents into always looking around the corner for a bogeyman. I can think of little worse than the agony of having a child abducted, but not all children reported missing have, in fact, been kidnapped. In 1985, a Pulitzer Prize–winning series of articles by Diana Griego, Lou Kilzer, and Norm Udevitz of the *Denver Post* revealed that many missing children were either in the hands of noncustodial parents or were runaways.[9] We need to do everything we can with government policy to restore these children to the homes that will best care for them. We should not, however, create a national hysteria based on seriously overstated numbers because that would be counterproductive.

This is not to deny that the press has been very helpful. The national coverage of cases like that of Lisa Steinberg, the six-year-old girl from New York City whose adoptive father is accused of having beaten her to death, or the allegations of sexual abuse at the McMartin preschool in Manhattan Beach, California, has dramatically called attention to the tragedy of abuse. Front-page stories can galvanize people into action and shock them out of their apathy. In my congressional office, I get many more letters on child abuse after such cases reach the public. People want to know how this can happen in our society and what they can do to ameliorate this national disgrace.

In the Child Abuse and Protection Act, we tried to set up a system by which trained people could identify children and parents who were in trouble and offer them help. The legislation was a catalyst for the expansion of a nationwide system of laws and agencies to protect children. Unfortunately, in many cases that system is now as vulnerable as the families it seeks to help. Child protection authorities are buckling under from the weight of too many cases and not enough resources. Investigating reports of battering, sexual molestation, or neglect is a difficult and delicate job—the stress is high, the pay is low, and the consequences are serious. People's lives can hinge on the judgment of the social worker assigned to their case. Yet some states don't even require social workers to have specialized training in their field. All professionals in this field are overburdened. In California, for example, the recommended caseload is sixteen families. The average caseload? Thirty-three families.[10]

In most states, social workers are required by law to investigate all calls concerning alleged abuse within twenty-four to forty-eight hours and to assume that every complaint is a legitimate one. Agencies have not been able to keep pace with the flood of reports. In 1986, social workers in Virginia investigated twelve thousand more complaints than in 1980, but identified three thousand fewer abused and neglected children. The sheer number of cases forced them to cut back on the thoroughness of their investigations.[11] The system is further hindered by a high turnover of caseworkers. For example, in New York City, staff turnover at Child Protective Services was almost 70 percent in 1987.[12] These problems cause gaps in the child protection system that can mean the difference between life and death for some children. Several studies suggest that in 25 to 50 percent of child abuse cases the family's problem was previously known to local agencies but no action was taken.[13]

Child protection agencies have another serious problem to contend with—the absence of clear direction from the courts on how to proceed with child abuse cases, and how to deal with allegations of sexual abuse in child custody battles. Changing the legal system can take a long time. Judges have to be educated, evidentiary rules have to be improved, and appropriate witness roles for minors have to be developed. The stakes in these cases are high. Even if an accused person turns out to be innocent, he or she has been stigmatized. False allegations can block mothers from adopting children, as well as prevent fathers from obtaining custody of their children.

Acknowledging the problems created by false reports, Congress passed the Child Abuse Prevention, Adoption, and Family Services Act of 1987, which called for a National Clearinghouse for Child Abuse and Neglect to make available standardized data on false, unfounded, or unsubstantiated reports. The bill also tied states' eligibility for grants to their efforts to encourage more accurate reporting.

Allegations of sexual abuse in custody battles have become more frequent over the past several years, and they pose particular difficulties for judges, who have to decide which allegations are valid. The judge becomes a referee in a bitter fight in which the father and his battalion of experts are pitted against the mother and her battalion of experts. All the while, the judge must try to determine what is in the best interest of the child. In a case in Alexandria, Virginia, for instance, a prominent surgeon, Dr. Elizabeth Morgan, accused her husband, Dr. Eric Foretich, of sexually molesting their daughter. He denied the charge and made the countercharge that his wife was emotionally unstable. Each brought out experts to counter the other's accusations. When the courts dismissed the case for insufficient evidence and granted the father unsupervised visitation, Dr. Morgan hid the child. She was jailed for contempt of court for refusing to reveal the whereabouts of her daughter, and as of this writing, she remains in prison. The child remains in limbo.

Public recognition of child abuse has opened the door for a more candid discussion of another sensitive family problem—spouse abuse. Studies show that the correlation between the two is very high—that child abuse frequently occurs in families where spouses, most often mothers, are battered. From my conversations with the medical community in Denver, I was familiar with a Colorado study that found that 53 percent of battering husbands also abused their children. The cycle of behavior that so often leads to child abuse is just as common in domestic violence—sons who see their parents fight are ten times more likely than other men to become abusers themselves.[14]

As with child abuse, the statistics concerning domestic violence are alarming. The FBI has estimated that a spouse or lover is beaten every eighteen seconds in this country. About six million women are battered each year. Between two thousand and four thousand die from injuries sustained in domestic quarrels.[15]

I have visited many battered women's shelters and have met with courageous women who left their homes despite threats by their husbands that they would eventually find them and kill them. This unfortunately is what happened to a woman in Denver who was divorcing her husband, whom she accused of beating her. During the proceedings the husband drew out a gun, killed his wife, and permanently paralyzed her attorney. Fear for their own safety and that of their children is one of the reasons many battered women do not leave their husbands. Women stay in violent relationships because they have little or no money, because their family and friends convince them that things can change, because they feel that they deserve the abuse, or because they simply have nowhere else to go.

Some tragic examples of spouse abuse that have been in the news recently have given a glimpse not only of the problem but also of how it cuts across class and cultural lines. In New York, there was the case of Dianne Pakul, whose husband, a Wall Street stockbroker, strangled her just as she had made plans to divorce him and start a new life. In Washington, D.C., we were stunned by the case of Charlotte Fedders, the wife of a top-ranking Securities and Exchange Commission official, whose husband beat her severely.

In 1979, the House first considered the Domestic Violence Prevention and Services Act, which requested $15 million to be used for grants to states to fund shelters and direct services for battered women and their children. The bill was defeated on the House floor, amid the opposition's cries that it would strain the federal budget and interfere with state, local, private, and religious programs, and that more domestic violence would result. One member even went so far as to call it "crap" and suggested that those calling for more help for women whose husbands beat them were anti-family.

In the debate, Rep. Elizabeth Holtzman, who was my predecessor as cochair of the Congressional Caucus for Women's Issues, said, "The opponents talk about the American family. This bill is designed to strengthen the family; we want to preserve human dignity, and we want to preserve human life. We want to deal with the serious problem of violence that can destroy the members of a family and that extends beyond the home to catch others in its grip."[16]

The Domestic Violence Prevention and Services Act finally passed in 1984. But conservatives, especially those in the Reagan administration, kept trying to thwart it. It took two years and a tremendous amount of congressional pressure to get the Department of Health and Human Resources to write regulations to implement the new law. One of the bitterest fights was over a $625,000 grant the Department of Justice was to give to the National Coalition Against Domestic Violence, an umbrella organization for most of the battered women's shelters in the country, to develop a model program for assisting victims of spouse abuse. Conservatives complained that the coalition was really a front group for feminists and lesbians and insisted that Attorney General Edwin Meese withhold the grant. On behalf of the Congressional Caucus for Women's Issues, I sent several letters urging Attorney General Meese to release the funds. He did, months later and only after reducing the grant by $50,000.

The next year, the Department of Justice awarded a grant that made further mockery of congressional efforts to help battered women. The Reagan Justice Department gave a Phyllis Schlafly spin-off group, the Task Force on Families in Crisis, $622,905 to educate the public on family violence, as well as to study the effects of domestic violence on "traditional women."

This seemed to me an attempt by conservatives to get even with feminists and to assure Phyllis Schlafly that the Justice Department had not sold out to the feminists. It made me angry. Here was an administration that had cut funding for treatment of child and spouse abuse in the name of the federal deficit, and now, for political reasons, it was squandering what little money we had left. The bogus group was formed solely for the purpose of receiving this grant, had no experience working with domestic violence, and did not even believe that battered women should have the opportunity to leave their homes. They were oblivious of the fact that, for many battered women, going to a shelter is the first step in breaking out of an abusive relationship. Schlafly said her organization got the grant simply because the administration "wanted to be fair and give a grant to a non-feminist organization to balance out one that went to feminists last year. . . . Fair play required equal treatment of traditional women."[17]

Social attitudes that get in the way of our acknowledging that there is such a problem as child abuse have also hindered the criminal justice system from responding to wife-beating as the criminal act it is. But judges and criminal justice officials are slowly being educated on the subtleties of domestic violence, and police and other law-enforcement agencies have become active in finding strategies to deal with it as a serious crime. The federal government has provided funds for more training in the effective handling of such cases. The police department is usually the first and only public agency to intervene in domestic quarrels and assaults against family members. Complaints of domestic violence are the calls American police departments receive most frequently. Police have found that the best deterrent for spouse abuse has been an aggressive arrest policy. The National Institute of Justice, in an experiment in Minneapolis, implemented a mandatory arrest policy for domestic disputes that has apparently led to a significant decline in spouse abuse. The mandatory arrest policy is now being used by hundreds of police departments. Similar success has been reported in those cities where mandatory arrests are augmented by immediate counseling of both spouses.[18]

In addition to family violence and the abuse and neglect of children, Congress has grappled with problems of alcoholism, teen suicide, and drug abuse. These problems are too complex and, unfortunately, too widespread to be discussed within the scope of this book. However, they are a catastrophe for the families that experience them. Individuals cannot cope with such burdens alone. They need practical and skilled help. A "Just say no" campaign is not enough. The Select Committee on Children, Youth, and Families has held extensive hearings on these subjects and the effects they have on family life. We have learned that there were over five thousand teen suicides in 1986; that alcohol is a contributing factor in family violence, divorce, delinquency, and suicide; and that alcoholism is the number-one health problem among young people. Drug abuse, especially with the recent availability of "crack," has seriously damaged the quality of life of our communities. Recent polls show that drug abuse is one of the major concerns of most people in this country.

There are many stressful periods that families have to endure: losing a family member, making it through economic hard times, caring for a seriously ill child or parent, relocating to a new community, dealing with emotional problems and substance abuse—even having a new baby. What can or should government do to help during such times? We've talked about such things as trying to ease the burden of working parents by providing them with day care and giving them more flexibility through unpaid, job-protected leave for family crisis. We've talked about instituting a fairer tax policy so that families have more after-tax income with which to build a better life. There is little argument about helping small businesses, areas that have suffered a natural disaster, farmers, and others essential to America's well-being. On that basis, nothing is more essential to a society than strong families. I think government has a special responsibility to assist families who are at the point of collapse. If they need special services to help them get back on their feet, those services should be available. Yes, that is compassionate, but it is also economically sensible. It is very expensive to take care of families that fall apart. Institutionalization, drug abuse, crime, homelessness . . . these are the conditions that drain America's spirit as well as its pocketbook.

Government must tread carefully. Government should be helpful but not intrusive; we should increase public awareness but not fan public hysteria. Family problems are dealt with best at the community and local level. Family law is primarily within the jurisdiction of the states. But it is the responsibility of the federal government to make sure that the states have adequate resources to provide services for people who need them, to fill in funding gaps, and to coordinate and communicate success. It was frustrating during the Reagan years to see spending cuts that forced the elimination of a vast number of the working poor from eligibility for needed social services. These actions produced an environment that increased the stress on families. Our national statistics reflect what the untreated and undealt-with stress got us: many more serious problems for society to deal with—in future budget periods and at much greater cost.

9

A National Family Policy

To be successful, a politician has to be good at communicating with the public. There is no better training ground for developing this skill than your own daily family life. You learn the give-and-take of human relations, how to put things diplomatically—as when I tell my children their rooms look like a bomb went off in a K-Mart store, for example. How to phrase things with the vividness necessary to get through to a child who is not studying for his final exams is always a challenge, as is surviving the daily crunch at the breakfast table. One morning a few years ago, I stood scrambling some eggs in my kitchen, thinking with irritation about how President Reagan seemed to escape unscathed from all of the failures and scandals of this administration. A moment later, when I looked down at the Teflon frying pan I was wiping clean, my face broke into a grin. That's what the Reagan presidency was like! Nothing stuck to it—not mounting deficits, trade imbalances, huge cuts in domestic programs, or even the scandals among the staff. *Ronald Reagan was a Teflon-coated president.* I couldn't resist the phrase, and later that day I trotted it out in a speech on the House floor. At least the term stuck—so to speak.

Helping my kids with their homework, arranging for the plumber to fix the washer, figuring out what to do about the raccoons in the attic, or researching summer camps with my children—all these experiences have kept me grounded as a person. Whatever our public role, it is our family chores, responsibilities, and joys—not politics—that form the core and rootedness of our lives.

I've been pretty open about the problems I've had balancing the separate parts of my life and I think that has made people less guarded with me. They tell me about their own complicated lives and they seem to empathize when I describe the times all the balls I was juggling dropped from the air at the same time. Everywhere I see the relieved reaction when people recognize their own problems in mine. For example, not long after Scott was born, Jim's sister, Sandy, and her husband came to visit with their children. When they were about to leave, Sandy took me aside and told me how relieved she was to discover that we were having the same problems with child-rearing as they were. There is so much pressure on families to produce perfect children and be the perfect family; we hate to confess we all harbor doubts about whether we are good parents or not.

The challenges I faced as a parent have been just as rigorous as those I had to deal with as a congresswoman. Campaigning every two years is tough, but so was seeing my son through his high school football career. Scott was always a rough-and-tumble kid. His first word was "dirt," not "mother" or "father." He had a set routine he would perform whenever we visited friends, and I learned to dread it. Scott would walk into a room, plant his feet solidly in the middle of the floor, look around to make sure he had people's attention, and then scream at the top of his lungs, "DIRT!" I never learned to laugh at it and the people we were visiting weren't exactly thrilled at this kid's one-word assessment of their homes. The fact of the matter is, if you want to see a dirty house, come see mine. I've always had a doormat announcing, "Dull women have immaculate homes," to prepare people as they enter.

Scott played football all through high school. It scared me to death, but Jim kept reminding me that if Christopher Columbus hadn't had a father he would not have discovered America, because his mother would have said, "Don't go, Christopher!"

Through my experiences as a "football mom," I learned a lesson about politics—the average person doesn't pay a lot of attention to it. During football season, I would wash and dry Scott's practice uniform every night so he'd have it clean for the next day. Once, when our dryer broke (washer-dryer problems have been the bane of my domestic life), I became a temporary regular at the local laundromat. The state of Virginia, where we live when we are not in Denver, was caught up in a governor's race that year. Charles Robb was one of the candidates and someone had left copies of his campaign brochure in the laundromat. The brochure included a photograph of the candidate with television personality Phyllis George. People coming into the laundromat would look at the picture one by one, then ask their friends, "Who is that with Phyllis George?"

Just as most people don't figure politics into their daily lives, politicians don't factor family issues into their legislative agendas. In one respect, the well-being of the American family is the most noncontroversial issue in American politics. Republicans and Democrats alike claim to be pro-family, never hesitating to mention their personal family values and to display family photographs prominently in campaign literature. But ask most politicians what they think about family policy particulars and they begin to shuffle their feet, wag their tongues, and steer the question back to their own families.

When I first ran for Congress, my opponent in the primary made much of the fact that his wife accompanied him on the campaign trail and that they had ten children. Then he would point out that *my* spouse was not campaigning with me—trying to raise suspicions about my marriage—and that I was not at home with my kids—implying I was a bad mother. Jim was not with me because we both felt it was better for him to keep the homefires burning. I always wondered who was home with my opponent's ten kids. For all his "family values," he never did address the real problems of parents and children in our district.

Such political pontificating remains the norm. The family gap—the difference between what politicians say about families and what they actually do for them—grows larger every campaign season.

It seems to me that one reason candidates don't address family issues is that most of them are insulated from the hassles and stresses of family responsibilities. They don't understand the everyday experience of the average American family because they don't live it. In lobbying different members of Congress about family issues, I've noticed that the only ones who "get it" are men who have become grandparents and have witnessed the dizzying pace of their children's lives; young men whose generation clearly expects both men and women to shoulder child-rearing responsibilities in marriage; and women who have had to balance career and family obligations.

There are also sharp disagreements about what the American family is and should be. I define "family" as Will Rogers did: "Family is where you go at night and they have to let you in." But, as we've discussed earlier, some people have a real need to believe in a family ideal that our economy makes rarer everyday: Mom at home, cooing the babies to sleep; Dad at the factory, whistling while he works. Others advocate the two-career household, a family structure not everyone wants. To speak about family issues, politicians first have to define them. That means running the risk of alienating some voters. But to keep the subject amorphous and utter melodious platitudes, warm fuzzies, as I call them, makes the family a safe issue, a non-issue.

Political courage is becoming a rare trait. Politicians increasingly rely on polls and pundits to tell them where the people are. The cloakroom wisdom is "There go the people. Let's scamper to get in front of them because we're their leaders." Family issues don't confer power on their advocates. Family issues aren't as prestigious as defense and foreign policy. Charting America's international destiny sounds like a more powerful cause than ensuring that fathers pay their child support. Wanting the best education possible for your child, caring for a sick child, needing to attend both a meeting at work and a child's school function, and trying to get by on a tight budget—these are the concerns of most constituents. Family issues aren't exciting, they are merely the stuff of everyday life. Washington, D.C., sees itself as the capital of the world's most powerful nation. A person who talks about family issues is perceived as dealing with the mundane, not with power.

There's an axiom in politics that voters don't want to hear bad news. Ronald Reagan's success in the 1980s with happy talk about "morning in America" seemed to prove this axiom. I disagree. Americans are an optimistic and pragmatic people who understand that until you look at a problem objectively, you can't remedy it. Constant happy talk is like a steady diet of cotton candy. Only after we have what I call a rendezvous with reality and acknowledge our present needs can we create policies that offer hope.

The government should initiate the debate, but if it does not, American families can turn the situation around by taking the offensive themselves. They must deliver a message to their elected leaders that it is time to make family problems a priority issue for action and for funding. That is how we will nurture and guarantee our position in the world in the next century. The twentieth century was often called the American century. What will the twenty-first century be called? What will America's role be?

The question of funding seems to cause the most anxiety. As I travel around the country pushing for family legislation, people say, "Sure, the family needs more help. But our country can't afford it. It costs too much."

Every politician knows there are always more good ideas than money to pay for them. Public enemy number one for American

families is the federal deficit. In order to remain a healthy, productive society we have to deal with our debts. On the other hand, the answer to the deficit problem does not lie in cutting programs that have proved successful. The truth is that a country's budget is the best reflection of its priorities. While it does take money to help families get off to a strong start, it costs much more to deal with families that crash. The huge federal deficit is used as a reason for not allocating money to family programs, but the bottom line is that our families are so important that we have got to figure out effective ways to promote their well-being. We must act now or we will have to pay much more later for having shirked these responsibilities. When financial objections to school programs are raised, I always say to myself, If you think education is expensive, try ignorance.

In 1988, a nationwide poll conducted for Kidspac, a children's advocacy group, indicated that people were willing to pay higher taxes if the revenues would go directly to such family policy components as childhood health and education programs.[1] I don't think higher taxes are necessary yet. We already have, in other departments of the government, funds that could better be used. For example, there is little doubt that we can find money in the defense budget that could be used for family initiatives. Recent disclosures about scandalously wasteful and corrupt purchasing procedures point to one way of freeing money for other purposes. We should take a serious look at whether we are getting our money's worth for the billions of dollars we spend in the name of defense.

Because the stakes are so high and the needs of our families are so great, we must all participate in the defense debate, rather than leaving it to the "experts." Sometimes we are too intimidated by experts; we are afraid to be beginners. Nobody wants to play tennis until they look professional, but how else can you learn? We must wade into the public debate on how our money is being spent and what we get for the expenditures.

During my tenure as a member of the House Armed Services Committee I have tried to demystify defense terminology as well as the defense budget process. Defense has always been a large part of the federal budget, with good cause, since national security is one of the basic functions of government. But because most of our tax dollars are spent for defense, we need to understand how defense proposals become budget priorities and therefore have a profound effect on the quality of our lives.

We can reduce the amount of money we spend without sacrificing the quality of our defense. Where does the money go? What do we get out for it? Are there better ways to accomplish what needs doing? We ask these questions about our modest family budgets; we should ask them about the huge national budgets that are driving us to the international poorhouse. "No budgetary sacred cows" should be our cry.

The military-industrial complex was the clear economic winner during the Reagan years. Ronald Reagan successfully campaigned for the presidency by blaming our budget problems on welfare queens—people who fraudulently obtain welfare benefits. But the blame rests more appropriately on the shoulders of defense contractors who cheat our military by overcharging or selling faulty equipment. If one welfare mother misuses her change from a dollar bill, the entire welfare system is called into question. But defense contractors who routinely charge $6,000 for a coffeepot or $700 for a toilet seat are merely scolded. The real welfare queens are in the military-industrial complex. Wasting the taxpayers' money at a time when we have such a high national debt and so many pressing needs is gambling with our future.

Waste and cheating are not the only problems. We must also question national priorities. The best warning came from President Dwight Eisenhower, who said: "We are not concerned merely with protecting territory, our people abroad, even our homes; we are concerned with defending a way of life. This, my friends, we must do by strength, a conciliatory spirit, and under-

standing, and with the cooperation of our friends in the world. It means that we must also defend that way of life always at home."[2]

President Eisenhower's words inspired me to pursue what I consider the reform that may hold the greatest promise for changing how we allocate our defense money and resources—burden sharing.

The concept of burden sharing is simple. It calls upon our allies to share both the responsibility and the financial burden of defending the free world. Burden sharing could profoundly change how we relate to our allies and how we allocate our defense dollars. We have struggled with the issue of how much our allies should pay for their defense since the 1950s, when NATO was formed. In fact, not too long ago I discovered a paper Jim had written for a foreign policy class at Princeton in 1957. Its title? "Why Our Allies Should Do More."

The problems of our present economy force us to reexamine our military commitments to the defense of other countries. As our deficit soars, our domestic policies unravel. We are doing ourselves grave injury. We can no longer afford to bear the lion's share of the burden of defending our allies.

Just as the American family has changed owing to changing economic forces, so also has the global family. Our developed allies are no longer struggling to recover from the chaos of World War II. The United States helped them to rebuild, and we helped our enemies as well. It had been a long and costly war but instead of going home, which we wanted to do, we stayed. We borrowed billions of dollars and gave aid to everyone, including countries that had been killing our sons a short time before. Unprecedented—and typically American!

Uncle Sam was an appropriate nickname for the United States in 1946, when we were giving assistance to so many nations. But the world has changed. Many of these countries no longer depend on us for their economic survival. In fact, they are undercutting ours. It is time *they* paid for their defense needs, not us. The

North Atlantic Treaty Organization was meant to be an alliance
to which each member contributed what it could afford, not a
reliance on the United States to do it all.

In 1988, the chairman of the House Armed Services Committee, Rep. Les Aspin from Wisconsin, appointed me to chair the
Defense Burden Sharing Panel, whose charge it was to explore
the cost and benefits of U.S. military commitments, to gather
facts about our interests around the world, to assess threats to
those interests, and to examine the extent to which our allies help
us to address those threats.

Cutting through the statistical clutter revealed the great extent
to which we currently subsidize our allies' defense. In 1981, President Reagan initiated a $1.4 *trillion* military buildup. In each year
since then, 60 percent of our defense budget has gone to NATO
defense commitments. While American military spending rose in
real terms by 5.7 percent from 1978 through 1985, our allies didn't
increase their defense spending by even the modest 3 percent they
had agreed upon.[3]

According to Congressional Budget Office figures, the United
States annually spends an estimated $1,115 per citizen for defense,
whereas France spends $511, Britain $488, and West Germany
$435.[4] That means, in effect, that each year out of *your* family
budget comes $1,115 per person for defense, of which 60 percent,
or $669 per person, goes to NATO. Would that be your choice?

A large part of the burden will fall to our children. They will
have to pay the cost of the national debt. They will have to
compete in a global economy. Yet today, domestic programs that
benefit children have been cut, and our kids are not testing as well
as children in many other countries. The heritage we are leaving
them is a huge debt—without the tools with which to pay it.

In 1984, the U.S. military budget was 212 percent of the combined military budgets of the fifteen other NATO countries.[5]
The cost to us of defending Western Europe in 1987 alone was
$171 billion. *That is more than our domestic deficit.* Western

Europe's combined gross national product is larger than our GNP, and its population is larger by a hundred million people. This policy of protecting equals and jeopardizing our own future is crazy.

Japan also fails to pull its fair share of the defense burden. It spends a little over $100 per citizen annually for defense, versus our $1,115. Americans admire Japanese technology—popping videos into Japanese VCRs and jogging to Sony Walkmans—but we hate the fact that the Japanese seem to be "kicking the stuffing out of us" in trade. The Japanese economy is booming in part because its resources and talents have been targeted to new technologies for consumer goods, not to defense. We spend 7 percent of our gross national product on defense. Japan spends only about 1 percent. What is worse, this 1 percent includes a number of "abstract" costs we would not count, such as tolls *not* paid by members of the American military. They also count "lost opportunity costs for land"—I *think* that means they're writing down as a "defense cost" a mythical amount they might have received from land the United States uses for bases to defend Japan.

Comparative figures on domestic spending are also shocking. Our allies spend much more per capita for education and health than they do for defense. Japan spends ten times as much for health and education as it does for defense. Not a single NATO country assigns a higher budgetary priority to defense than to the health and education of their citizens. We do. *We spend more on defense.* Even more telling is the way we spend our research-and-development (R&D) money. The NATO countries spend two thirds of their R&D budgets for health, education, the environment, and other concerns of the civilian sector and only one third for military applications. Our spending is the reverse: over two thirds for military R&D and only one third for civilian R&D.[6] I can't prove there is a connection between what Japan spends on health and education and the impressive statistics on the progress of Japanese children, but it seems very logical. Furthermore,

Japan's infant mortality rate has declined so much that Japanese people have the highest life expectancy at birth in the world. Between 1975 and 1985, the proportion of Japanese children living in poverty decreased by half, from 25 percent to 12 percent. *During the same period, the poverty rate for American children rose from 19 percent to 24 percent.* [7]

Our European allies have some of the most progressive family policies in the world. Whether it is child care, parental leave, or health insurance, their citizens enjoy a wide range of family benefits. People come up to me and complain that they don't want any of their tax dollars going to national health insurance or day care. They are surprised when I tell them that they already pay indirectly for these things—for citizens of other countries. The money that we save our allies by paying for a hefty portion of their defense enables them to enact the progressive and comprehensive family programs that we Americans do not have and think we can't afford. When I travel to Europe to talk with allied leaders about burden sharing, they say, "If you make us pay more money for defense, we may have to raise taxes or cut services." "Right," I tell them. "That's exactly what we have had to do in the United States."

It is our children who have paid the price of our astronomical defense budget. Our country has higher rates of infant mortality, teen suicide, divorce, teen pregnancy, and alcohol and drug abuse than most of our allies among the developed nations. Recent polls show Americans want to curb defense spending and fund more domestic programs. The guns-vs-butter debate is as old as our country, for it goes to the heart of our founders' principles. Our forefathers did not want to be an imperial power. They were more interested in the welfare of our own nation. People like George Washington and Thomas Jefferson, who were themselves rich, fought for the right to bring others along who weren't as fortunate. The world had never seen a revolution like ours. That is our heritage. We forget that just one hundred years ago there was a raging debate about the annexation of Hawaii and the invasion of the Philippines. The choices we have made in foreign policy from World War I to the Vietnam War, extending our reach and the sphere of our influence, have affected our ability to live up to our principles at home. Our foreign policy has affected not only the way we spend our money but the nature of our democracy itself. We must inspire the democracies we helped to save to now share our world responsibilities so that we are not forced to undercut what is due to our own citizens.

We live in a world where the economies of many nations are interrelated; where regional conflicts can lead to superpower showdowns; where the superpowers no longer have a monopoly on sophisticated nuclear weapons. The global village is more a reality than most of us care to admit. We cannot retreat to the world Washington and Jefferson saw for us. But it is time to begin a new debate about our national identity. Who are we as a people and what do we stand for as a nation? What are our national values and how do we live up to them at home as well as around the world?

It seems clear to me that the changes in our country's demographics, family life, and economy make it imperative that our federal government provide leadership on family policy. This isn't a call for big government. Some of the most effective and successful programs include money-saving preventive initiatives, such as childhood immunization. Government action is not the prescription for all of America's family ills, but to underestimate the government's role is as bad as to overcommit and overregulate. To ignore the federal government's obligation to its families is to pass up a golden opportunity for this country to soar into the next century. That's why I call family policy the moonshot legislation of the 1990s—a national challenge that can inspire the entire country, just as getting to the moon did in the sixties.

In advocating a national family policy, I am in no way suggesting that states' rights be preempted. Laws that affect family life have been, and should remain, the primary responsibility of the states. However, a state-by-state approach by itself would result in disparities among states and uneven coverage for families across our country. Also, as in the case of child support, disparate state regulations allow people to move around and "shop" for ways to evade local regulations they don't like. Washington, D.C., should be providing minimum federal guidelines and financial support to states to implement their own laws.

A national family policy should have three basic goals: to acknowledge the rich diversity of American families; to protect the family's economic well-being; and to provide families with flexible ways to meet their economic and social needs. Government policy cannot be based upon a static definition of the family, but must take into account that Americans live in a variety of family structures throughout their lives. Two-parent family, single-parent family, blended family, extended family, and empty-nest family—each of these comes with particular stresses and needs. An understanding of this diversity is essential if we are to avoid creating government policy that penalizes families that don't fit a particular mold.

In this book, I have tried to identify those issues that a national family policy must address: fairer treatment in the tax code; family and medical leave; affordable child care; minimum health care coverage; retirement security; and a right to decide whether, when, and how to have a family. But these will simply remain laudable goals unless we can mobilize a constituency around them. In the past, the term "family issue" has been used by both conservatives and liberals as a shield behind which they worked for their traditional goals. The family constituency has never really developed an identity of its own with an appropriate and specific agenda. Women's groups; labor; those interested in welfare, children, or fundamentalist issues—all have spoken of "family issues" when they thought it would make their cause more palatable. The new family constituency should be a combination of all these groups, not specifically the property of any one of them. The goal should be to improve how the American family functions.

Out of the 1988 Great American Family tour that I took with Dr. Berry Brazelton, Gary Goldberg, and Diana Meehan, evolved the idea of the American Family Team, a project to make it possible for parents to lobby on family legislation at both federal and state levels. We need such efforts to counter special interest lobbies that invest heavily in defeating family-issue legislation. The coalitions that support work and family issues are out there, but they have not been mobilized to counter the much-better-organized forces that currently control access to money and power.

I know from my own experience how little time parents have, but even so, we need to push for a *family* lobby so that our voices will be as powerful as those of other lobbying groups. It is *not* hopeless. People who care *do* make a difference. We Americans are impatient and want immediate results from our labors. If we don't see change in thirty minutes, we assume we haven't made a difference and we drop out or retreat. But with persistent and consistent pressure, things can change. Demonstrations during the Vietnam War did have an effect. Ronald Reagan's 1988 visit to the Soviet Union, a nation he once characterized as an Evil Empire, would never have taken place had it not been for the rising call by Americans in support of such a move and of arms control.

My friend Elise Boulding, a professor at the University of Colorado, wrote, in an article entitled "Learning About the Future," that historically, American parents always used to think the world would be better for their children.[8] During the 1950s, the outlook began to change; parents hoped the future "wouldn't be worse than it is now for the next generation." Boulding observed that over the past thirty years, Americans have become pessimistic about their children's future.

The most compelling argument for urging our government to

create a national family policy is to improve the outlook for the future. We know how to do it. We know how we can pay for it. We've seen programs that work. Our government and our people should step out front together and make a strong moral and practical commitment to the Great American Family. It is our country's future that is at stake.

Notes

Chapter 3

1. The Alan Guttmacher Institute, "Abortion in the U.S.: Two Centuries of Experience," *Issues in Brief*, vol. 2, no. 4, p. 3.

2. The Alan Guttmacher Institute, *Teenage Pregnancy in Industrialized Countries* (New Haven: Yale University Press, 1986), p. 202.

3. National Research Council, *Risking the Future; Adolescent Sexuality, Pregnancy, and Childbearing* (Washington, D.C.: National Academy Press, 1987).

4. Office of Technology Assessment (OTA), Summary of its report *Infertility—Medical and Social Choices* (Washington, D.C.: Government Printing Office, 1988), May 1988, pp. 1, 2.

5. Ibid., p. 9.

6. Infertility Fact Sheet, House Post Office and Civil Service Subcommittee on Civil Service, Hearing on H.R. 2852, July 23, 1987, serial no. 100-22, pp. 75–76.

7. Testimony of William L. Pierce, President of the National Committee for Adoption, before the House Post Office and Civil Service Hearings on the Federal Employees Family Building Act, March 9, 1988, serial no. 100-40, p. 35.

Chapter 4

1. U.S. Department of Labor, Women's Bureau, "Standards for Maternity Care and Employment of Mothers in Industry" (Washington, D.C.: Government Printing Office, 1942).

2. "Women Who Maintain Families," U.S. Department of Labor, Women's Bureau, no. 86-2, 1986. And "Money, Income, and Poverty Status of Families and Persons in the U.S.: 1986," U.S. Bureau of the Census, *Current Population Reports,* series P-60, no. 149,

3. Dr. Janet Norwood, Commissioner, Bureau of Labor Statistics, Testimony before the House Select Committee on Children, Youth, and Families, April 17, 1986.

4. *The Parental Leave Crisis: Toward a National Policy,* ed. Edward Zigler and Meryl Frank (New Haven: Yale University Press, 1988), pp. 343–345.

5. Sheila B. Kamerman, Alfred J. Kahn and Paul Kingston, *Maternity Policies and Working Women* (New York: Columbia University Press, 1983).

6. "Parental Leave," Joint Oversight Hearing before the Committee on Education and Labor Subcommittees on Labor-Management Relations and Labor Standards, and the Committee on Post Office and Civil Service Subcommittees on Civil Service and Employee Benefits and Compensation, October 17, 1985.

Chapter 5

1. Children's Defense Fund, *A Children's Defense Budget, FY 1989: An Analysis of Our Nation's Investment in Children* (Washington D.C.: Children's Defense Fund, 1988), p. 186.

2. John Fernandez, *Child Care and Corporate Productivity: Resolving Family/Work Conflicts* (Lexington, Mass.: D.C. Health Company, 1986).

3. T. Berry Brazelton, M.D., *Working and Caring* (Reading, Mass.: Addison-Wesley Publishing Company, 1985).

4. Testimony of Paul Rupert before House Government Operations Subcommittee on Employment and Housing, "Rising Use of Part-Time and Temporary Workers: Who Benefits and Who Loses?," May 19, 1988, p. 139.

5. "Child Care: Key to Employment in a Changing Economy," Hearing before the House Select Committee on Children, Youth, and Families, 100th Congress, March 10, 1987, p. 3.

6. *Child Care Employee News,* "Child Care Workers: A Precious Resource," vol. 6, no. 3 (Summer/Fall 1987).

7. Children's Defense Fund, *A Children's Defense Budget, FY 1989,* p. 191.

8. "Opportunities for Success: Cost-Effective Programs for Children Update, 1988," a Report of the House Select Committee on Children, Youth, and Families, 100th Congress, p. 39.

9. Marshall Ingwerson, "Going to School at the Office: Company Builds Classrooms for Children of Employees," *Christian Science Monitor,* April 6, 1988, p. 3.

10. Dana E. Friedman, "Child Care for Employees' Kids," *Harvard Business Review Special Report* (March–April 1986), p. 4.

11. Testimony of Harry Freeman, American Express, before the House Select Committee on Children, Youth, and Families Hearing "Child Care: Key to Employment in a Changing Economy," 100th Congress, March 10, 1987, p. 55.

12. "Childcare, A Workforce Issue," Report of the Secretary's Task Force, U.S. Department of Labor, April 1988, p. 164.

13. Fred Barnes, "Baby Face-off," *New Republic,* May 9, 1988, p. 9.

Chapter 6

1. Sar Levitan and Richard Belous, *What's Happening to the American Family?* (Baltimore: Johns Hopkins University Press, 1981). Testimony of Tamara K. Hareven, "The Diversity and Strength of American Families," Hearing before the Select Committee on Children, Youth, and Families, U.S. House of Representatives, 99th Congress, February 25, 1986. Steven Mintz and Susan Kellogg, *Domestic Revolutions: A Social History of American Family Life* (New York: The Free Press, 1988).

2. Irwin N. Gertzog, *Congressional Women: Their Recruitment, Treatment and Behavior* (New York: Praeger Publishers, 1984), pp. 150–151.

3. United States Commission on Civil Rights, *The Equal Rights Amendment: Guaranteeing Equal Rights for Women Under the Constitution,* Clearinghouse Publication 68, June 1981.

4. "Problems of the Displaced Homemaker," by Tish Sommers and Laurie Shields, Alliance for Displaced Homemakers, Women in Midlife—Security and Fulfillment, Part 1, A Compendium of Papers, Select Committee on Aging, U.S. House of Representatives, 95th Congress, December 1978.

5. Laurie Shields, *Displaced Homemakers: Organizing for a New Life* (New York: McGraw-Hill, 1981).

6. Lenore J. Weitzman, *The Divorce Revolution: The Unexpected Social and Economic Consequences for Women and Children in America* (New York: The Free Press, 1985).

7. Ibid, p. 36.

8. *The Washington Post,* October 22, 1984.

9. "Divorced Military Wives Seek Benefits Reforms," by Caryle Murphy, *The Washington Post,* October 22, 1984.

10. Testimony of Shirley Sandage, Executive Director, The Older Women's League, before the Committee on Education and Labor Subcommittee on Labor-Management Relations, U.S. House of Representatives, September 29, 1983.

Chapter 7

1. "American Families in Tomorrow's Economy," Hearing before the Select Committee on Children, Youth, and Families, U.S. House of Representatives, 100th Congress, July 1, 1987, p. 3.

2. "Preliminary Assessment of the Impact on Women of the Administration's Proposed Budget," The Women's Research and Education Institute of the Congresswomen's Caucus, March 30, 1981 (hereafter WREI Analysis).

3. Steven Mintz and Susan Kellogg, *Domestic Revolutions: A Social History of American Family Life* (New York: The Free Press, 1988), p. 240.

4. WREI Analysis.

5. Robert Greenstein and Keith McKeown, "The Decreasing Anti-Poverty Effectiveness of Government Benefit Programs: 1979–1986," The Center on Budget and Policy Priorities, Washington, D.C., 1987.

6. Gordon Berlin, "The New Permanence of Poverty," *The Ford Foundation Letter,* vol. 19, no. 2 (June 1988), p. 2.

7. Barbara Reskin and Heidi Hartman, eds., *Women's Work, Men's Work: Sex Segregation on the Job* (Washington, D.C.: National Academy Press, 1986), p. 4.

8. Irwin Garfinkel and Sara S. McLanahan, *Single Mothers and Their Children: A New American Dilemma* (Washington, D.C.: The Urban Institute Press, 1986), p. 46.

9. "Child Support Compliance," *The Urban Institute, Policy and Research Report,* vol. 18, no. 1 (Winter 1988).

10. Garfinkle and McLanahan, p. 137.

11. *The New York Times,* June 19, 1988.

12. Testimony of Donna R. Lenhoff on behalf of the Women's Legal Defense Fund before the Senate Committee on Finance on Title V of the Economic Equity Act, June 21, 1983.

13. Statement by Harry D. Krause, U.S. Senate Finance Committee, Subcommittee on Social Security and Income Maintenance Programs, Hearings on Child Support Enforcement Program, October 4, 1983.

14. Lenhoff, p. 3.

15. Reskin and Hartman, p. 4.

16. Ibid.

17. "Pay Equity: Equal Pay for Work of Comparable Value—Part I," Joint Hearing before the Subcommittees on Human Resources, Civil Service, and Compensation and Employee Benefits of the Committee on Post Office and Civil Service, U.S. House of Representatives, 97th Congress, September 16, 21, 30, and December 2, 1982, p. vii.

18. Reskin and Hartman, p. 10.

19. The 1988 Joint Economic Report of the President, Report of the Joint Economic Committee, U.S. Congress, April 20, 1988 (hereafter JEC Report), p. 37.

20. "Trends in Family Income: 1970–1986," Congressional Budget Office, February 1988.

21. "American Families in Tomorrow's Economy," Hearing before the Select Committee on Children, Youth, and Families, U.S. House of Representatives, July 1, 1987.

22. JEC Report, pp. 46–47.

23. *The Washington Post,* June 2, 1988.

24. Testimony by Deborah J. Chollet, Senior Research Associate, Employee Benefits Research Institute, before the Select Committee on

Children, Youth, and Families, U.S. House of Representatives, July 1, 1988.

25. *The Washington Post,* December 16, 1987.

26. Employee Benefits Research Institute, Issue Brief, June 1987, no. 67.

27. *National Journal,* March 14, 1987.

28. Testimony of Sen. Daniel Patrick Moynihan before the Select Committee on Children, Youth, and Families, "Tax Policy: What Do Families Need?," April 24, 1985.

29. Henning Gutmann, "The Bad New Tax Law," *New York Review of Books,* February 12, 1987.

30. *The Denver Post,* July 7, 1987.

Chapter 8

1. Douglas J. Besharov, "Doing Something About Child Abuse: The Need to Narrow Grounds for State Intervention," *Harvard Journal of Law and Public Policy,* vol. 8 (Summer, 1985), p. 542.

2. Frank Moya, "Legislators Discuss Child Abuse in Denver Hearings," *Rocky Mountain News* (Denver, Colorado), April 1, 1973, p. 28.

3. "Abused Children in America: Victims of Official Neglect," Report of the House Select Committee on Children, Youth, and Families, 100th Congress, March, 1987, p. 15.

4. American Association for Protecting Children, *Highlights of Official Child Neglect and Abuse Reporting, 1986* (Denver, Colorado: American Humane Association, 1988), p.2

5. Besharov, p. 551.

6. Testimony of Frederick Green, M.D., President of the National Committee for Prevention of Child Abuse, "Child Abuse and Neglect in America: The Problem and the Response," Hearing before the House Select Committee on Children, Youth, and Families, 100th Congress, March 3, 1987, p. 17.

7. "Abused Children in America," p. 212.

8. American Association for Protecting Children.

9. Diana Griego, Lou Kilzer, Norm Udevitz, "The Truth About Missing Kids," *Denver Post,* May 12, 1985, p. 1.

10. Green, p. 24.

11. David Whitman, "The Numbers Game: When More Is Less," *U.S. News and World Report,* April 27, 1987, p. 39.

12. Testimony of Suella Gallup, AFSME Local 371, New York, before a joint hearing of the House Select Committee on Children, Youth, and Families and the House Ways and Means Subcommittee on Public Assistance and Unemployment Compensation, Child Welfare, Foster Care, and Adoption Assistance, April 13, 1988 (unpublished).

13. Green, p. 18.

14. House Select Committee on Children, Youth, and Families, Fact Sheet on Domestic Violence, citing Murray A. Straus, Richard J. Gelles, and Suzanne K. Steinmetz, *Behind Closed Doors* (New York: Anchor Books, 1980).

15. Testimony of Elizabeth Holtzman, District Attorney, Kings County, N.Y., "Women, Violence, and the Law," Hearing before the House Select Committee on Children, Youth, and Families, 100th Congress, September 16, 1987, p. 37.

16. House Debate on H.R., 2977, December 12, 1979, *Congressional Record,* p. 35554.

17. Mary Deibel, "Schroeder Attacks Granting of Funds to Schlafly Spin-off," *Rocky Mountain News* (Denver, Colorado), June 5, 1986.

18. Holtzman, p. 41.

Chapter 9

1. Peter D. Hart Research Associates, Inc., "Key Findings from a National Survey Conducted for Kidspac," June, 1988.

2. Remarks made by President Dwight D. Eisenhower, Public Papers of the Presidents of the United States: Dwight D. Eisenhower, 1958. Washington, D.C.: Government Printing Office, p. 799.

3. Congressional Budget Office, "Alliance Burden Sharing: A Review of the Data—Staff Working Paper," June 1987, p. 15.

4. Report of the Defense Burden Sharing Panel of the House Committee on Armed Services, 100th Congress, August 1988, p. 24.

5. Testimony of Paul F. Walker, Codirector of the Institute for Peace and International Security, before the House Armed Services Committee Panel on Defense Burden Sharing, March 16, 1987 (unpublished).

6. Walker.

7. Dr. Samuel Preston, Unpublished remarks at the conference "Children at Risk: Who Will Support Our Aging Society?," sponsored by Americans for Generational Equity, Denver, Colorado, May 1988.

8. Dr. Elise Boulding, "Learning About the Future," *Bulletin of Peace Proposals,* Universitetsforlaget, Oslo, Norway, vol. 12, no. 2, 1981.

Index

About the Author

PATRICIA SCOTT SCHROEDER represents Denver, Colorado, in the House of Representatives. Representative Schroeder, first elected in 1972, is the dean of the women in Congress and cochair of the Congressional Caucus for Women's Issues. Schroeder sits on the House Armed Services Committee, the House Select Committee on Children, Youth, and Families, the House Judiciary Committee, and the House Post Office and Civil Service Committee, whose Subcommittee on Civil Service she chairs. She also cochairs the House Armed Services Task Force on Defense Burden Sharing.